THE GIRL
WHO BITES HER NAILS

and

THE MAN
WHO IS ALWAYS LATE

What our habits reveal about us

Ann Gadd

FINDHORN
Press

© Ann Gadd 2006

First published by Findhorn Press in 2006

ISBN 1-84409-073-6

British Library Cataloguing-in-Publication Data.
A catalogue record for this book is available
from the British Library.

Edited by Kate Keogan
Cover design by Damian Keenan
Interior design by Pam Bochel

Printed by WS Bookwell, Finland

Published by

Findhorn Press
305a The Park, Findhorn
Forres IV36 3TE
Scotland, UK

tel 01309 690582/fax 690036
info@findhornpress.com
www.findhornpress.com

To Ruth and Stan,
with gratitude and love

Acknowledgements

I am deeply grateful to all the people whose stories helped me to understand various behaviours. To the many sources that appeared just when I needed them, I am most grateful. To Anthony, Tess and Taun for their understanding, support and love and for all those friends and family who encouraged me along the way. Also to my publisher, Karin Bogliolo, for those wonderful words 'I am sitting here with a huge grin on my face...', which reverberated across continents to make the book a reality. A special thanks to those teachers who knowingly and unknowingly have taught, inspired and expanded my thinking. Thank you.

Table of Contents

Section 2 – Examining Actual Habits

Introduction

You meet life's philosophers in strange places. Take Bert, the owner of a hotel in a remote area of the Transkei on the east coast of Africa.

I had retreated from the hot African sun into the bar where Bert was settling into a lager, a habit, judging by the size of his gut, to which he was very partial. 'You know,' he said, after taking a pensive slug out of the bottle, 'you would not believe how many tourists come to the hotel and never leave the grounds.'

That surprised me – how could one come all this way and not explore the beautiful surroundings? For in spite of an adventure that had at times been simply uncomfortable and at other times plain terrifying, we now felt hugely exhilarated. We had conquered our fears of the surrounding unknown.

We had set out on what was loosely called a road, but which was in actual fact a series of pot-holes joined together by mud and rocks. We had been accompanied, after one really deep pothole had forced us to stop, by at least twenty local villagers, who scrambled inside the Landrover and, when this was full to burst, onto the roof and bonnet, to enjoy the free ride. This made visibility for the driver something of a problem, particularly down the tricky 60 degree incline. Later, we went for an oppressively hot walk through bush which was home to thousands of hungry insects who had been waiting for months for unsuspecting tourists. And then there was the matter of the four-foot snake swimming alongside me across the lake... .

I could now understand why the hotel held a magnetic appeal. How many of us never explore the outer world for fear of experiencing what we would rather avoid? Likewise, we would rather relax alongside our emotional selves than delve deeper into their workings, believing that somehow this makes us happier individuals.

Understanding is seldom comfortable. The more we understand, the less able we are to adhere to our old ways of being. While discovering new aspects of our physical world may be challenging, discovering more about our emotional world can be disquieting. Consequently, this book may be difficult to read. It takes courage to confront our shadow sides and often we are not prepared to do so, reacting with denial and hostility to ideas that threaten the image we have created of ourselves.

Our shadow is where we have hidden all those parts of ourselves that we find unacceptable, or that society or our family tells us are not okay. We carry it around with us, often unconscious of its very existence. And yet it peeks painfully through our behaviour, when we least expect it to. So, like the majority of tourists at Bert's hotel, we ignore exploring and hope that by avoiding the discomfort, it will disappear.

Yet it is in our shadow side that the gold often lies. And it is through working with these issues and releasing them that we find true peace and wholeness. Like our foray into the African bush, it is not always a comfortable journey, but the reward of becoming more conscious is well worth the effort. You may read about your habits or ways of acting and get irritated with the insights, denying their validity. This is mostly because they may mean that you realize the need to change and, as we know, change to most of us is about as exciting a prospect as an ice-cold shower in winter!

Life is more than the daily struggle to make a living. It is about finding our authentic selves, the wholeness *(holy-ness)* of who we are. Yet to reach this realization, we often have to sift through the layers of calcified perceptions and understandings about who we are. This book is a tool to assist you in this process.

There may be some of you who choose not to work with the contents of this book. And that is fine. But for those of you who do have the perseverance and courage to do so, may the journey bring you to a place of deeper understanding, compassion, joy and delicious peace.

Section One

Habits: An Overview

Chapter One
Habits and why they develop

A momentary impulse, an occasional indulgence, a passing whim may by repetition become a habit difficult to uproot, a desire hard to control, and finally an automatic function that is no longer questioned. By repeated gratification of a desire, a habit is formed, and thus habitual conditioning can grow into compulsion.

Nyanaponika Thera[1]

We may lie, constantly lose our keys, procrastinate, bite our nails, battle to be punctual, snore, play with our hair, drink too much coffee or smoke twenty cigarettes a day.

Most of us reading the above list would have identified with at least one of the examples, if not most of them! All of these habits, together with many hundreds not listed, may be irritating or even detrimental to our health in the long term, but seem to ease our tension in the short term. When we are feeling uptight, sad or angry, a quick fag or nail-biting session often helps release the stress caused by the emotion, even though we may regret having done so later. This you will acknowledge if you smoke and have to walk up five flights of stairs or if you have to hide your hands on a date after an energetic nail-biting session.

Yet we still persist in repeating the same pointless and harmful behaviours, seldom questioning why we do so. Even the threat of losing a job, a close relationship, our health or the respect of others, seldom persuades us to change.

We all repeat behaviour that is harmful to us, be it on an emotional, mental, spiritual or physical level. Those of us who do admit to our harmful habits need not feel alone. In my years of working with people, as a counsellor and alternative practitioner, I have yet to meet one person who does not have some form of negative habitual behaviour. At this point, many of you may want to protest that you don't have any behavioural defects. Maybe you don't chew things, have addictions or deviant sexual habits. But before you polish that halo, ask your partner, friends, family or colleagues what habits you have and you could be in for a big surprise!

You may be blissfully unaware that you speak too loudly, scratch your crotch while thinking or that you sniff often and play with your nose hair. Many of the people I interviewed for this book were very surprised to find out that they did have habits of which they were not really aware. While you may not have an addiction to obvious habits such as tobacco, narcotics or alcohol, you may need to have three spoons of sugar in your tea, find it hard to resist chocolate or are addicted to being sweet and polite instead of voicing the anger you actually feel.

Why is habitual behaviour so intrinsic to our existence? What's the point? Until now we have largely overlooked, denied or ignored our habits, yet as the mind-body connection becomes more understood, we have to acknowledge that there must be a connection between what we do physically and what we feel emotionally.

See-saws and swings

Let's imagine that our emotions resemble a see-saw. When the see-saw is parallel to the ground, it is perfectly balanced. When the see-saw is tilted to extremes, one end is high (on a high) and the other is down (or depressed). Issues with people or circumstances that cause strong emotions are what upsets our balance. The greater the weight or burden of these issues, the less likely the see-saw is to remain parallel to the earth or in balance and, consequently, the more likely we are to experience mood swings, instability and persistent negative emotions. When balanced, we are calm, despite what is happening in the rest of the playground we call life.

Each time we try to balance the see-saw, some person or event drops a ten-tonne load on the one end and *boom!* – we are left with a skewed outlook (and see-saw,) that has us feeling completely stressed, despite all the yoga, breathing exercises, meditation and lentils we have been attempting to do/eat in order not to reach this state. When stressed, drained and emotionally-exhausted, we inevitably revert to all our old habits and replace the Lentil Surprise with a Big Mac and Coke, or yoga for the pub, in an attempt to feel better. The trouble is, the behaviour just pushes the one side of the see-saw further into the ground and no amount of waiting for the 'right person', job or lottery win to sit on the other end and balance things out produces either the person or the desired goal.

All of this stress eventually burns us out and then we find that we lack the will, energy or desire to work with the real issues that are causing the see-saw to swing wildly from one side to the other. So we give up and comfort ourselves, as we sit down in the dumps, with whatever habit we have chosen.

This book is about recognizing the issues that cause our see-saws to lose balance and, by understanding these issues, helping to swing things in our favour.

The good, the bad and what is ugly

We all have two aspects of ourselves: the one that acts according to our conscience and the other that defies or disregards it. You know the feeling when you've already eaten five pieces of chocolate and this 'Bad' voice says:

'Have that last piece of chocolate, even though you've eaten nearly the whole slab. Go on; it'll taste divine and it's a pity to waste it on the kids.'

To which the sound of your conscience, or 'Good' voice, replies: *'No I shouldn't really. It's not good for me.'*

To which comes the reply: *'Oh, come on; live in the moment. Enjoy! Forget about your weight loss program. One more piece won't matter.'*

And so it continues back and forth whether it's over something as minor as chocolate, or as major as defrauding the company for which we work. Our habits are no different and are an indication that the 'bad guy', or lower self, within us is running roughshod over our higher ideals.

We want to be fit and healthy, yet cannot stop eating junk food and smoking. We want to be someone whose word is truth and yet each sticky situation finds us lying our way out of our responsibility. If we are going to grow into better human beings, then we need to confront this shadowy aspect of ourselves.

It's because we don't want to acknowledge that we have lost the perpetual battle that we ignore the 'good guy's' plea of long-term gain and revert to the wonderful acceptance and short-term gain of the 'bad guy'. Afterwards, we feel ugly or guilty, which creates stress which we need to alleviate and so are spurred on to continue the cycle. Habits, through their very repetition, are a great way of understanding how we are limiting ourselves from being happy, healthier human beings.

To illustrate how insight into our habits can help to heal us, here is an example from a woman who had heard me speak about habits. She wrote me an email to let me know what her experience had been, once she had understood her problem to a greater degree.

Sue was an attractive, thirty-something brunette, who had been a PA in a large accounting company until she had stopped working to care for her two young children. She had married a man she had met in her final year of school, and the marriage appeared to be happy, although communication was sometimes an issue. While outwardly calm and composed, her raw, red nail-beds and jagged, torn nails indicated that all was not as well as it outwardly appeared. For as long as she could remember, Sue had bitten her nails. No amount of expensive treatments had proved to be remotely successful. The unsightly nails were the price she had come to pay for a few moments each day of relief and the satisfaction of biting. She had come to see me on another matter entirely when the conversation turned to her nails.

When she read my first book, *Healing Habits,* Sue immediately related to the issue of suppressed anger which is part of the reason that we nail-bite. 'Whenever I used to get extremely angry and resentful with my husband, kids or mother-in-law, I'd chew my nails. A favourite time was when I watched television, was stuck in traffic or when I had nothing better to do with my hands. I had, however, never learnt to join the dots, i.e. my anger with my nail-biting. When I came to understand and later observe my behaviour in a detached manner, I was able to feel the connection.'

'Having understood that my nail-biting and suppressed anger were linked, I set about determining to deal with or confront the issues and people that angered me when they arose. I'd approach each person I was angry with and tell them how I felt, as opposed to avoiding them and fuming silently. Sometimes, with my newly-acquired ability, I did lose my temper and go over the top, which was perhaps not ideal, but it certainly brought the issue to their attention. With my husband I'd point out that, unless the behaviour changed, there would be no sex, going out or any other thing that he wanted me to do. At first, I was very afraid that by doing so I would chase my husband away and fail to get the approval of those around me. I have, though, now that much of the initial wave of anger has been expressed, learnt how to say what I feel, without needing to use harsh or angry words.'

Sue had a very demanding and manipulative mother-in-law who used to rule her with an iron rod. From what food to cook, to her personal life, the old lady attempted to control the household. Many weekends would find Sue at home looking after the critical woman, while the rest of the family was out enjoying themselves. Sue also confronted this issue: 'I told my mother-in-law exactly where she could take her criticism of me and put it ... . Needless to say, she DID NOT like that and I got a blistering phone call the following morning. Later, I told my husband categorically that, unless she apologized to me for what she said, she was no longer welcome in my home... . (Yes, *my* home!) As a result, I have had nothing to do with her since then. It has been very, very peaceful, but I still can't help thinking that it is the calm before the storm. However, I feel very much better equipped to handle any situation that may arise.'

'I realize now how much I was manipulated through fear of angering or upsetting anyone or not being the perfect wife/mother/daughter-in-law.

'Funnily enough, telling everyone how I feel has actually worked! My family now think that I've changed and maybe they preferred the old resentful but timid me. My husband even accused me of being menopausal! The new 'expressive' me doesn't impress him one little bit, but I am no longer going to accept everything that is dished out to me so submissively. It's not that I am actively going out to look for fights: it is just that I am no longer going to accept the mental abuse. It's so *simple* really; after all these years, I have realized that I don't have to accept it. Getting rid of my frustration took away all desire to nail-bite as well as stopping the sharp, stabbing pain I had been getting in my chest – often followed by a severe headache.'

'Now, on Sundays when watching television, I do a complete manicure and, of course, that helps the nails even more. I am still working with general stress in my life by walking on the treadmill at the gym and by doing deep-breathing exercises which really do help.'

Sue decided to take up a friend's offer of a weekend away. Before, she would have been too afraid to ask to go, but with her new found sense of power, she went. 'It was a truly wonderful break and I felt that I had had a holiday even though we were only away for two days and one night. My family coped extremely well without me, and my nails still look beautiful.'

Another case of recovery from a habit is that of a man in his forties who snored. Sean drove his wife to distraction with his humongous racket each night. A holiday with the extended family proved disastrous, as other family members complained about a lack of sleep due to Sean's snoring which vibrated loudly throughout the wooden house.

Feeling conscious of the disturbance he was causing, Sean went through a series of special pillows, throat sprays, snoring plasters, herbal preparations and vibrating wristbands – to no avail. Sean and his wife were desperate. 'It wasn't simply a loud, peaceful snoring but rather one that built up to a crescendo before abruptly stopping, only to build again. It wasn't what you might call a major turn on,' reported his wife.

Snoring, as you'll discover in Chapter Five, is related to blocking new experiences, resisting change, and the resulting anger with ourselves, or with others whom we may see as hindering our ability to change or move forward.

Sean was, at the time, in a business partnership that was full of problems, but which he seemed unable to take any action to resolve. His partner seldom did any work and yet received a higher income. If weekend work was involved, it was Sean who did it; if business travel was required, Sean sat in the back of the plane in tourist class while his partner lavished in business class. All but one of the staff reported to Sean, who dealt with their daily problems and issues arising from employing staff. Meanwhile, his partner read magazines.

To add to this already unbalanced partnership, Sean was pretty convinced that his partner was stealing from him. Yet he still took no action, because he feared being able to run a business alone. Rather than confront him and risk the partnership's breaking up, he chose to remain silent. He was angry, both with his situation and with his inability to alter it. To avoid actually dealing with the way his life had evolved, Sean developed a keen fondness for alcohol, which only increased the snoring, as did the extra weight he was carrying.

As so often happens when we are resistant to change, life springs some surprises on us that force us to accept it. Sean was no exception and, when the degree of theft became so large and undeniable, he was forced to take action. This he did and, after a lengthy battle, at last he shed his scheming and deceitful partner. Suddenly alone at the helm, he realized that he was quite capable of running the company single-handed and of making the changes he had wanted to implement.

As he did so, his need for alcohol lessened, (although he still drank), his snoring subsided and eventually all but disappeared. Since then he has made more changes to his life, each time realizing that the more you do it, the less frightening change becomes. His need to make the harsh, snarling sound we call snoring was removed, not simply because of his alcohol reduction, but because he no longer felt anger and resentment towards his partner. He had removed the need to be angry with himself and to warn others to steer clear of trying to change him and the situation.

Sean heard me speak about snoring and its emotional issues at a talk I was giving on habits and later came and spoke to me, saying that he related extremely well to the emotions I had described. 'I had always wondered just why I had stopped snoring. There seemed no rational explanation. I still drink, I'm a bit overweight and yet I seldom, if ever, snore. The logical explanation is that it has stopped through my understanding of where I was and where I've grown. Funnily enough, though, my wife has started to snore! Perhaps I can support her to make the changes she is afraid to make!'

Habits and patterns

Whenever we have a negative habit (as opposed to a positive habit, such as meditating), it is an indication that we are no longer in balance and that some aspects of our lives are not functioning as well as they could.

It is as if in their repetition our habits remind us of where we have become stuck in the past and where we need to clear issues in order to live fully in the now. Let's say, for instance, that when you were young you were told by one or other parent that you would amount to very little, which made you feel small and insignificant. Now, you may have long forgotten those actual words, but the program remains. Just as you are about to succeed at something, that 'being insignificant' program comes into play and you (most likely unconsciously) create an obstacle or event that arrests your progress. You may drink too much at the office cocktail party and insult the manager's wife, thereby putting paid to your eminent promotion. You may delay (procrastinate) completing a vital report and consequently lose an important new client, or you may resort to bragging about your achievements in an attempt to impress – with the opposite result. The behaviour you choose is not that important: recognizing the pattern is. Becoming aware of these programs through understanding your habits helps you to become more fully conscious of who you are and what programs no longer serve you. This awareness then offers the potential to grow beyond your past programming.

Habits as helpers

When our co-worker keeps spilling coffee all over the place, when our child keeps bed-wetting, or our spouse constantly criticizes us, we may be at a loss to understand why they are doing what they are doing. This can make things confusing and, consequently, we may react in ways which we later regret. The Native Americans are reported to have said that, until you walk a mile in another man's shoes, you cannot judge him.

Using the information in this book, then, is an excellent way to understand why someone is acting the way they are. In reaching a greater understanding of them, you may find that you can be more compassionate towards them and assist them to help themselves with a particular issue. You achieve far more that way than by gossiping about them to your co-workers.

BE WARNED. It is one thing to seek to understand someone else and their issues (whilst acknowledging your own) and to help them discover this for themselves. It is quite another matter to spout forth to an intrigued audience the personal details of why so-and-so is doing what they are doing. Telling your superior in frank terms that their habit of belittling others is simply a mask for their own pathetic inadequacies will neither win you friends nor influence anything other than your own demise! Use the information contained in the later chapters to *enlighten yourself* rather than dim the spark of others. Don't expose people's 'stuff' unless they specifically ask for your insight and, even then, do so with compassion and caution.

Endnotes

[1] Nyanaponika Thera. www.buddhanet.net

Chapter Two
Stress and habits

Broadly speaking, we can cite stress as the overriding emotional cause of negative, repetitive behaviour, but stress itself can be caused by many factors – such as fear, resentment, jealousy, anxiety, and so on. It is these underlying causes that result in the stress. Stress is a broad brushstroke: it is the finer, emotional detail that causes us to behave in particular ways.

In this book we will examine not only stress but, more specifically, these underlying emotional reasons from which the stress arises. By doing this, we can not only come to a deeper understanding of our habits, but also of ourselves. Understanding why we do things makes it easier, then, to observe the triggers and stop or lessen the behaviour. Stress in itself is not what causes the habits: rather, the emotions that lead up to our experience of life as stressful are the root cause. We get stressed over what we have suppressed, as opposed to expressed.

Before we get into specific habits and their causes, let's examine the result of these emotions, namely stress.

Surging Stress Levels

Stress is when you wake up screaming and you realize you haven't fallen asleep yet.

Unknown

Our lives are, on average, far more stressful now than they were in the past. Psychiatrist Richard H. Rahe M.D. conducted a study published in London that showed stress has increased, on average, by 45% in the past thirty years. Additionally, in another study of 5000 British managers, the concept of a job for life simply does not exist in our world, where mergers and restructuring result in retrenchments being commonplace. Of the 5000 managers interviewed in the research, 61% had had to deal with organizational restructuring in the year of the survey.[1]

The anger and repressed aggression that they were largely unable to express, together with feeling completely powerless, not only increased stress levels but, in many instances, manifested as depression.

When CEOs are at play engineering new and improved companies, those who are not part of the process are left feeling completely disempowered. They feel that they have no control over what happens in their lives – it is as if they are mere pawns on a large corporate chessboard, where a high level of work performance does not guarantee maintaining your job.

In 1990, a Labour Force Survey in Britain revealed that one percent of the population was suffering from work-related stress, anxiety disorders or depression. Just five years later, the percentage had risen to 30%, and if the scale were to continue, as it undoubtedly has, the percentage would now be even higher. Average annual absenteeism per individual case due to stress and depression exceeded that due to any musculoskeletal disorders (28 vs 19 days).[2]

But it is not only those who face retrenchment who are under significant stress: certain types of job are also prone to causing a greater degree of stress. Those particularly at risk are people who work in jobs such as the police, fire and prison services, where physical danger causes constant stress. These occupations are followed (in order of number of individuals affected) by health and social welfare associate professions (such as dentists, doctors, paediatricians or nurses in casualty), skilled construction and building trades, teaching and research professions, and skilled metal and electrical trades.[3]

Having to perform a number of different jobs at the same time is stressful, particularly when those roles clash, such as for a mother who works from home. Trying to cope simultaneously with the demands of a three-year-old and meet a client deadline is extremely stressful. New employees who are unsure of what is expected of them find life stressful and even a supposed positive occurrence, such as a promotion, can cause stress. Interpersonal demands, inappropriate management styles and a lack of understanding between personalities can cause a huge amount of work-related stress. Peer or group pressure – where the employee feels obliged to act in a certain way or to have to live up to the expectations of others – can also place huge pressure on the individual.

Another cause of stress is your environment. If you work alone, in an office that's very crowded or which lacks privacy, or where the temperature is too hot or cold or the noise levels are high, you may find your stress levels rising. A study in the *Journal of Applied Social Psychology,* by Laura Cousin Klein, associate professor of bio-behavioural health at Penn State University, found that women who were subjected to high levels of noise in the office, such as phones ringing constantly, printers clacking away and colleagues speaking, became understandably frustrated and were later inclined to eat more fatty and comfort foods (twice as much) as the women who had not become so frustrated. Klein said that, *What's interesting is that during the noise during work, people rise to the occasion. They accomplish the job they have to get done, and they do quite well at it. They block all the other things that are going on their environment out. But there's a psychological and mental cost to that, and after that's over, once the stressor is done, then we see this behavioural element.*[4]

This is precisely how our negative habits work. Emotional responses that we suppress – whether they are from environmental factors, people or situations – lead to stress, which we often release through habits. The greater the suppressed emotions, the greater the incidence of habits.

But it's not only in the workplace where stress levels have increased. At home, the traditional family structure is in the process of disintegrating with more and more single parents finding themselves alone with the awesome responsibilities involved with raising children. Not only that, but they have to juggle full-time jobs with children's needs, as well as their own. Inevitably, it is their own needs that end up being sidelined, which adds to the frustration and stress level as, when we aren't fulfilled, we literally feel empty. Being empty emotionally, we will seek someone or something to fill that emptiness, which may not be in our best interests. This is especially so if it is someone who takes advantage of our neediness and the situation becomes abusive, or else we may become addicted to a substance. This in turn will drive our stress levels skyward.

How do you know if you are highly stressed?

> *Your biography becomes your biology.*
> Carolyn Myss[5]

'You know you are uptight when you find yourself trying to set the office laser printer to stun,' reads a bumper sticker! Because of the ability (as described by Laura Cousin Klein) to switch off from our emotions in order to deal with the task(s) at hand, we are often not aware of how stressed we actually are until we have the first stroke or find ourselves with ME or some other type of debilitating illness.

Even then, we often fail to heed our bodies' warning signals, choosing to slowly destroy ourselves, rather than examine why we are so stressed/ill and try to do something about that. This was illustrated to me clearly when the husband of a friend of mine had a stroke. In spite of his doctor's orders, he insisted on returning to the office the very next day. Did he believe the office would fall apart without him for a few days? Or was it that he was afraid of spending time out and being forced to confront what had happened to him and its life-threatening consequences? I suspect it was probably both. Most of us are no different.

It's often helpful to run this list past someone with whom you live or work and get their input, as we can be masters of denial. One man I worked with was extremely controlling and stressed, but saw his constant calls to his wife to 'check up on her' as being caring rather than controlling. He also saw his desire for perfection in the way the household was run, (which drove his wife to distraction and his children to despair,) as 'caring for the home'. He mistook his frequent, angry outbursts and tirades as 'caring more for his family and household' than his wife did. His bouts of heavy drinking and drug-taking he classified as 'having a bit of fun'. This may be an extreme example, but the point is that we seldom see ourselves as others do.

Here, then, are a few warning signs that may assist you in recognizing your degree of stress:

- Having very high expectations of others
- Being overly-demanding of yourself and others and insisting on perfection
- Getting extremely frustrated with yourself and others when these perfection-needs aren't met
- Being quick to anger, intolerant and impatient
- Setting unrealistic goals that later feel overwhelming
- Judging yourself and others too harshly
- Using words such as *have to, should, need to, must* and *ought to* frequently
- Escapist behaviour and an increase of negative habits

In a famous American study from 1967, Dr. Thomas H. Holmes and Dr. Richard H. Rahe created a do-it-yourself stress test. They numerically rated stress-causing experiences ranging from the death of a spouse (100) to getting a traffic ticket (11). By adding the values of these experiences from the past year, you can predict the likelihood of stress-related illness or accident.[6] However, what Drs Holmes and Rahe did not take into account is that people respond to similar situations differently. Some may see the loss of a job as a major tragedy, from which they battle to recover for many years, while others may view the same job loss as an opportunity to explore a field they had always wanted to, but felt afraid of taking the first step. For these people, although carrying some fear, the challenge might outweigh the concern.

In the workplace, a certain amount of stress is essential if we are to find our careers stimulating. For instance, a highly-intelligent professor would be more likely to feel stress from having to repeat a similar task every working hour than he would if he were snowed under with more stimulating work.

Interestingly enough, middle-management suffers more heart attacks than does top management. This is no doubt because top management feels in control when it comes to decision-making, whereas the staff lower down the pile are implementing top management's decisions, whether or not they believe in them. They are also more likely to be constantly judged and criticized by those above them.

How much stress we experience, then, is directly related to how disempowered we feel.

Victim versus victor

If we do not take responsibility for our lives and consequently feel like victims of others' actions and behaviour, we will feel more stressed. An empowered person realizes that things can go wrong in the world around them; because they feel empowered, they feel enabled to act and alter what is appropriate, in order to lessen the negative effects of the experience. A disempowered person, however, will remain in blame and feeling that the responsibility is in no way theirs, and will be less inclined to take action to avert or negate the results of events.

A person who has much personal power and who finds their spouse cheating, may instead of only blaming the silly old cow/idiot, actually be able to examine what in their own behaviour may have contributed to the situation. Perhaps they were too involved at work and have started to ignore their partner; perhaps they had not always been caring and attentive; maybe they had become too serious and the fun and spontaneity had disappeared from the relationship. Such a person can then work with these issues, accept their part in the demise of the relationship and then forgive both themselves and their partner and move on from the experience.

The stress, then, will undoubtedly be there, but it will be far shorter-lived than that of the disempowered person who, in not owning any responsibility, may spend years plotting revenge, blaming the partner, loathing the partner's new love and generally making life hell both for themselves and all concerned. They see themselves as the innocent victim of all that has occurred. As victims are those who have things *done* to them (passive), they are less likely to want to take action and move on from the situation. Consequently, the stress for them may continue for years, long after their ex has happily moved on. Holding onto their pain/wound, then, has become the elixir that gives them reason to exist. Consequently, telling such a person to move on will not be met with appreciation; rather, you will be lucky if your knee-caps still face forwards!

For such a person, learning to own the responsibility for their actions then becomes the path to their healing and personal power. It is a long and arduous road where we frequently slide back unless we are super-vigilant; however, the reward is less stress and consequently better health and lifestyle.

The actual word 'stress', comes from the Old French *destresse*, based on the Latin *distringere* meaning to 'draw apart'. When we are stressed, we are literally being pulled in different directions. We talk about being financially 'stretched' or 'stretched to our limits'. Being stressed or stretched means we do not feel whole: we feel fragmented, shattered and torn apart.

Eliminating stress

Most of us encounter stressful situations throughout the day – whether it's driving to work and being stuck in traffic for an hour or having to care for a sick child. In this we have little choice; however, *we do* have choice in how we respond to these situations. Is our whole day ruined because someone gave us the finger for responding too slowly to a traffic light, or can we laugh his actions off and forget about the situation minutes later? Here are some ways to work with ridding ourselves of stress.

Delegation

It is easy enough to say, but much harder to actually do. Delegating means giving up control to a certain extent and it's for this reason that we often shy away from it. We would rather get totally stressed out and work until all hours of the night simply to feel that we are in control of the outcome. This gets back to the need for perfectionism mentioned earlier. And who better to produce the perfect result we require than ourselves!

Why do we dislike delegating? It's not just the less-than-perfect result we fear, but rather the fear of not being in control. We have become distrusting of life and people and therefore our outlook is coloured with the certainty that the only person we can trust is ourselves. This is, of course, absurd and relates strongly to a diminished ego that seeks gratification. We create our own stress by telling ourselves that we alone are capable. So often people behave like this in the workplace, especially, yet, miraculously, when the time comes for them to leave the company, it continues to function extremely adequately!

All the hours of extra labour and the resentment that came with it are then to no avail, save for stressing us out and making life difficult for those around us. Realize, then, that when you believe that only you can do something well, it is your ego and fear that is controlling you. By starting to trust others, to have faith in their abilities and to empower them, you take a huge step in authentically empowering yourself, as well as lessening your long-term stress level.

Many people do try to do this but, in not genuinely trusting those to whom they have delegated, they incur even greater stress through constantly worrying about how things are progressing. Letting go means just that – trusting that the task will be done well, even if the way it is performed is not exactly what you had in mind.

Taking a break

Many of us avoid taking breaks, be they holidays or 15 minutes of relaxation, because we are concerned that a) no one will notice our absence and realize we are not critical to the functioning of the organization, for example, or b) because we can't let go of control.

If we do take a short break we either pump ourselves full of caffeine or nicotine, both of which increase our stress level, or devour a sandwich while downloading our email, neither of which is calming. Rather than calm you down, these things are stimulants which make your heart work harder and increase your blood pressure. Instead, take a short walk, relax and breathe deeply, or stare out of the window for a few minutes – anything, just to take your focus away from the stressful situation.

Prioritization

Many of us increase our stress levels because we avoid doing certain tasks that we find less appealing or difficult. This may be an awkward phone call, a project we don't feel sufficiently competent to do or a routine task that is simply boring. (Procrastination is covered in greater detail in Chapter Twelve.) By setting out a specific plan of action and prioritizing tasks, we keep ourselves from avoiding facing the tasks we don't want to do. The satisfaction we feel afterwards, when the tasks are completed, and the reduction in stress is well worth the effort.

Express rather than suppress: if you have grievances with someone, tell them. Leaving it to fester will only make it worse for you and them. Most people would prefer to have you say what is troubling you than have you walk around silently under a massive storm cloud of anger. If you have a problem at work, for instance, and have tried to follow the company grievance procedure without success, you will probably not be enjoying your job anyhow and, rather than live in this stressful situation, hating each day, it may be time to consider a change.

Sport

It is important to remember, though, that engaging in a sporting activity should be a way to relax. Don't fall into the trap of allowing your competitive nature to surface and thereby ruin an event that may otherwise have been fun. Now is not the time to beat yourself up if you didn't win. Use the time as a way to meet new people and share some laughs.

Spontaneity

When did you last do something different? Not just wear a pair of shoes you haven't worn for a long time, but something unexpected and that you didn't plan? Doing something like having a picnic in the park, trying out a new restaurant with a type of food you have never eaten, going to a dance lesson, going for a country drive to an area you haven't been to – these can all create new excitement and get your focus off the stressful situation for a few hours.

A relaxing home

Make your home your haven. Make your home or apartment the sort of place that you want to return to. Keep clutter to a minimum and ensure that you have tranquil music at hand. Share the day's events with your partner, but be careful of falling into the trap of competing with each other for who had the worst day. This can reach a point where in order to 'win', you can overlook all the good things for the sake of winning the 'feel sorry for me' prize. Having someone who listens to you recall events of your day can help to let them go, but remember this is reciprocal.

Equality

The belief that all people are equal creates a huge amount of discontent and creates stress as we may desire what someone else has and blame ourselves, or others, for not achieving what they have. Nature is not equal – the eagle flies higher than the dove, the rose is more beautiful and has a finer smell than the dandelion, the jungle is more fertile than the desert. Yet we persist with the myth that we are all equal and therein lies much of our discontent. Some of us are short, others tall, some attractive, some ugly, some fat, some thin, some wealthy, some impoverished, some wise, some less so, and so on. By accepting our inequality and yet striving for our own personal best within our limitations, we drastically reduce the stress that envy, attachment and blame cause.

So love yourself for who you are, unconditionally, and don't wait for the day when you are wealthy, wise, slim, fit, etc. to appreciate all that you are.

Endnotes

[1] Dr Richard Rahe's website: www.drrahe.com

[2] The report, *Self-reported work-related illness in 2003/04: Results from the Labour Force Survey,* can be accessed at *www.hse.gov.uk/statistics/causdis/swi0304.pdf.* Musculoskeletal disorders, followed by stress, depression or anxiety were by far the most commonly-reported type of work-related illness with corresponding *prevalence* estimates of 1.1 million and 0.6 million for people ever employed. The ranking was reversed for *incident* cases, with an estimate of 0.2 million for musculoskeletal disorders and 0.3 million for stress, depression or anxiety. Furthermore, although the estimated *annual working days lost* were of a similar order for the two conditions, the average annual days lost per case was higher for stress, depression or anxiety (28 days) than for musculoskeletal disorders (19 days).

[3] The report, *Self-reported work-related illness in 2003/04: Results from the Labour Force Survey,* can be accessed at www.hse.gov.uk/statistics/causdis/swi0304.pdf Occupations carrying above-average estimated *prevalence* rates (for people working in the last 12 months) of work-related stress, depression or anxiety were: teaching and research professionals with an estimated rate of around 2.7% and business and public service professionals with an estimated rate of around 2.3%. Corporate managers (2.1%), health and social welfare associate professionals (2.0%) and business and public service associate professionals (1.8%) also carried above-average estimated rates. These occupational groups together accounted for around half the estimated prevalent cases of self-reported work-related stress, depression or anxiety (for people employed in the last 12 months).

[4] Laura Cousin Klein. From:
abclocal.go.com/kabc/health/070204_hs_noise_women_weight.html
Penn State University: 311B East Health & Human Development Building

[5] *Your Biography becomes your biology.* Caroline Myss Ph.D. From Daily Message Archive
myss.com/myss/dailymsarch.asp

[6] Dr. Thomas H. Holmes and Dr. Richard H. Rahe stress test:
www.aspexdesign.co.uk/psych_lifechanges.htm

Chapter Three
What is the difference between a habit, an addiction and Obsessive Compulsive Disorder (OCD)?

OCD is not common. In fact, only about 3% of adults have it and it is even less common in children (0.3-2%).[1] So, just because you like to check you've locked your car at least once or you wipe your kitchen counter down at least four times a day, does not mean you have OCD. With this in mind, then, let's examine more about OCD and how it differs from a habit.

As the name implies, there are two aspects of OCD: the obsession and the compulsion. Usually, but not always, people suffering from OCD display both.

What is an obsession?

An obsession is a recurrent and persistent thought, image or impulse that is intrusive, unwanted and inappropriate. When the obsession persists, has no apparent cause, makes the sufferer distressed and makes life difficult, intervention is needed. This does not refer to the recurrent worry you may have about losing your job, or whether your husband may be having an affair, both of which could be classified as real-life worries, excessive as they may sometimes become. Rather, with obsessions, it is as if the thought, image or impulse becomes 'stuck' and will only go away when the person follows some other specific action or compulsion. So the action or compulsion itself is only a *result*, not the cause. Often, the person will be aware that the original trigger for the action is simply a creation of their own mind, yet this knowledge is insufficient to dispel the thought, image or impulse.

However, there is a grey area between the habits that we may have and OCD. It is considered normal to have certain ways of doing things and this does not amount to OCD. For instance, we may drive to work a certain way for the benefit of passing a favourite site: we do not feel compelled to do so from a belief that failure to do this may result in our partner being involved in a terrible car accident. If we were to feel compelled to drive a certain route because not doing so would result in a car crash, for instance, such behaviour could then be said to be OCD.

Compulsions

The compulsion, then, is a reaction to the obsession and must be adhered to rigidly. Failure to do so will, in the mind of the sufferer, result in a major disaster or situation occurring. Forcing themselves not to follow the compulsion results in a huge increase in stress, which only performing the compulsion releases. By performing the compulsion repeatedly, the sufferer believes he or she will make the obsession go away. This then sets up a pattern of repeated behaviour. Even though sufferers may be aware that acting out the compulsion is illogical, it worked at reducing the fear and tension in the past and so they will be compelled to repeat the performance in order to feel relaxed again.

Certain fears seem to be more common than others, such as the fear of **contamination** from dirt and germs. Any surface or situation then holds huge fear in terms of possible infection, from AIDS to dreaded diseases; the sufferer may become extremely anxious if forced to touch something or someone that they perceive may infect them. The response to this will likely be a need to **wash** repeatedly. Such people may wash to the point of making their hands or body sore and inflamed.

Sexual behaviour may represent huge fear or no-go areas that confuse those who experience them. **Touching** others may become the chosen compulsion to alleviate the tension that these thoughts or desires have caused. A young man I knew felt compelled to stroke the arm of the person to whom he was speaking as a way of dealing with his obsessive, intrusive sexual urges.

Counting or **adding**, be it car number plates, cracks in the pavement or any other object which lends itself to being added or counted could be the result of obsessions relating to **religious** and **moral fears** of not behaving in an acceptable manner. It is most often silent and others may not be aware of what is happening. Because doubt is very much part of OCD, a person may feel the need to recount continually, in order to make sure that they counted correctly in the first place.

Symmetry, or arranging, is another feared situation, as was the case with a young girl I knew who feared much happening to her if she did not smooth down her bed in a certain way and lay out her teddies in an exact order, before she went to sleep. An adult may need to place possessions in a certain order or pattern in a room to fit into 'rules' to keep hidden thoughts and feelings under control.

They may have recurring fears about themselves or those close to them being involved in **horrific situations.** Imagining harming either themselves, as in self-mutilation (covered in Chapter Fourteen), or someone else can also be a very disturbing obsession. **Repeating** words, phrases or parts of poems may be a way of dispelling the obsession.

Perfectionism may be taken to extremes, where certain tasks have to be performed to almost unattainable standards. This need to be perfect causes a huge amount of stress which often is relieved by **hoarding.** (Hoarding is covered in greater detail in Chapter Ten). The need to be perfect may require working late into the night just to be sure that everything is 100%.

Ever wondered whether you have **locked the door** of the house or car and had to go back to check? That's a fairly common habit. However, if even after checking twice, you still keep doubting that you did check, or keep needing to go back long after logic has dictated that the house or car is secure, then you may be erring on the side of OCD. This need to check can also relate to assignments or projects that may be late, not because they have not been done, but simply because the information needs to be checked and rechecked in order to be perfect. This links in with the perfectionism mentioned above. This need to check can be a counter for **aggressive urges** or a fear of losing control of aggressive feelings and acting on them. Other habitual checking when taken to extremes – be it the amount of money in one's purse or whether the oven is switched off – can also be related to suppressed aggression.

If you know someone who has a constant need to **pray,** it could be that there is much hidden in their psyche that they need to **confess** or relate to another person. They may also need to ask certain questions and their resistance to do so (commonly through fear of what result the answer will bring) may lead to constant praying. It's a way of appeasing guilt or to ward off scary thoughts. It could also manifest as the need to tattletale on others – to confess other people's sins and hide their own. There are no set rules, however, and these examples are simply common ways in which compulsions manifest.

How do I tell a habit from OCD?

OCD differs in one very notable way from a habit in that the actions do not give the person performing them any pleasure. They simply relieve tension and the fear which results from the discomfort of the obsession. Having a few pints at the pub every Friday may be a habit or an addiction (depending on the amount consumed) but it is, nonetheless, enjoyable. Procrastinating or nose-picking may not necessarily be hugely enjoyable, but the act does give a certain amount of pleasure, even if it is only to show the office how little you think of the project you've been given to complete, or to allow you to breathe more freely. With OCD, the only payoff is the relief from the obsession.

The symptoms of OCD impact heavily on the sufferer's life and may affect their job performance or relationships and cause huge distress. Most OCD sufferers are aware that it is their own minds that are the cause of the problem (which is not so with the sufferers of many other psychotic disorders, such as schizophrenia). This can be very disturbing. In some instances, the symptoms may be mild and may come and go while, with others, they may be far more frequent.

To **summarize**: **OCD** comprises an **obsessive thought/idea/impulse**; a reaction or **compulsion** to do something in response to that thought/idea/impulse; and the fear which performing the compulsion will allay. A **habit** is simply a regular tendency or practice that may be hard to give up.

Healing OCD and when to get outside help

Research suggests that, in terms of brain chemistry, insufficient serotonin levels may be a cause of OCD and that brain circuits appear to return to normal after taking serotonin medication or receiving cognitive behavioural psychotherapy. Communication problems between the front part of the brain and the deeper basal ganglia have also been cited; however, there is no single proven cause of OCD.

It is disturbing that OCD often goes unrecognized. According to the *Obsessive Compulsive Foundation,* studies show that it takes an average of seventeen years from the onset of OCD until the obtaining of appropriate treatment.[2]

Because sufferers may keep it a secret and because it is not widely understood, or access to appropriate treatments is not always available, OCD is often undiagnosed. This is a pity as, with proper treatment, patients can avoid suffering and lessen the risk of developing further problems (such as broken relationships or depression) which can result if the OCD is left untreated. Treatment can bring about long-term, symptomatic relief in many people; others may be fully curable.

On Drs Holmes and Rahe's stress test (mentioned in Chapter Two), revision of one's personal habits received a rating of 24, only one below a major change in living conditions (such as rebuilding) and one above having trouble with a boss. Eliminating a habit is not an easy task;

understanding why you developed it in the first place is of greater assistance to you in ridding the underlying cause than is simply trying to fix the resulting behaviour.

Improvement is possible and in some cases a full remission is experienced.[3] Consequently, it seems worthwhile to seek intervention should you be concerned that you or someone you know has OCD.

How do I tell a habit from an addiction?

The word 'habit' comes to English from the French and means 'a condition, dress, demeanour or appearance'. This word derived from the Latin *habere* (from the Indo-European root *ghab*) meaning 'to have, hold or possess'. If we combine the two meanings, a habit is a condition, dress, demeanour or appearance of which we take hold. The word is also used in a religious context to imply that the outer habit worn by monks and nuns reveals their inner, spiritual conviction. They 'have, hold or possess' their beliefs.

Just as a nun's habit demonstrates her inner convictions, so our personal habits give us an idea of what is going on in our inner selves or subconscious. Our habits, as repetitions of our behaviour, highlight our emotions. There are hundreds of different habits that we perform, from blushing to bragging, yet we have probably never questioned why we behave as we do. By recognizing our habits, then, we can come to a greater understanding of ourselves or, as Aristotle said, '*we are what we repeatedly do.*' (*Nicomachean Ethics* c. 325 BC)

Habits are performed often with little or no conscious thought. They do not have quite the same power over us as addictions do and, in most cases, with a little effort we are capable of limiting if not stopping them. An addict, however, has much more trouble giving up his or her vice, even when health, finances and relationships are affected. A heroin addict may want to give up, but to do so will entail a far greater degree of discipline, courage and willpower than will giving up nail-biting, for instance, hard as that might be to stop.

The word 'addict' comes from the Latin *addictus* meaning 'given over' or 'devoted to'. In the modern sense it is associated with rewarding or devoting oneself to something or with yielding to a particular practice. By yielding to this practice, we reward ourselves with a sense of well-being. It is often associated with a substance, such as nicotine or opium. It is a physical as well as emotional craving, whereas a habit is more like a mirror for an emotional need.

How habits are formed

Most of us have little outlet for the stress which we all experience to some degree. So habits become a way of acting out the neurosis which is the cause of the original stress.

Whatever form the habit takes, then, is linked to what makes us uptight. It may be anger, fear, resentment, jealousy, anxiety, or any number of other emotional triggers. We may do something consciously (or more often unconsciously) and find that it helps to lessen the emotion, and so we will naturally be inclined to repeat the action the next time we are under the same pressure. Before long, the behaviour has become an ingrained response to a particular state of being and follows a cycle as shown below.

In the example below I have taken the need to clean a surface more than once. Let's say it starts with a housewife who is experiencing anger and resentment towards her husband, whom she experiences as abusive and belittling. This causes huge resentment and anger within her which she is afraid to express. She does not want to face up to the fact that her relationship is unhappy and that there are serious problems in the home. She wants everything to appear to be just fine. Literally, on the surface everything needs to look good. So she cleans and re-cleans to make everything sparkle – except of course for herself, who is far from sparkling. This is how her cycle might manifest:

- **Trigger emotions:** anger and distress repressed

- **Guilt:** for feeling so angry

- **Self-esteem issue:** not expressing her anger and allowing her husband's words to make her feel small eats at her self-esteem/willpower

- **Sadness:** this makes her sad and she grieves for the loss of her old, confident self

- **Truth and denial:** she is still not honest with herself as to the extent of her relationship problem

- **Result:** performing the habit makes her feel better as at least she can do something well and feel some sense of achievement, and things appear to look all right on the surface.

Let's examine the way a smoker may unconsciously experience the emotional need to light up:

- **Trigger emotions:** need for stimulation. Fearful and anxious

- **Guilt:** for smoking so much
- **Self-esteem issue:** knowing you are reliant on a substance that you can't give up eats at self-esteem – shame at lack of self-control
- **Sadness:** sad that you are hooked on a habit
- **Truth and denial:** denial of the extent of the problem: 'I only smoke twenty a day,' when in reality it's more like thirty
- **Result:** have a cigarette to reduce tension

There is an upside to this exercise:

Recovering:

- **Understanding**
- **Insight**
- **True nature of addiction**
- **Love of self**
- **Increase in self-esteem – feeling empowered**
- **Working with feelings as opposed to avoiding them**
- **Good health and vitality**

Next time you catch yourself eating too quickly, indulging in some intensive retail therapy or procrastinating while there is still time, run through the list above starting with **trigger emotions** and work your way through the **recovering** list to examine your habit in greater depth – you could just learn a lot more about yourself.

Why learning more about ourselves is useful

There is a saying that goes *'the first page of the book of life is a mirror'*. By understanding ourselves we can start to understand the nature of all things, because we are the microcosm while the universe is the macrocosm or, as the Bible states, *'As above, so below.'*

By examining our physical bodies and their disease we can understand our emotional bodies and their dis-ease. The very reason that these emotional aspects became subconscious or hidden in the first place is that they mirrored to us aspects of ourselves which we deemed not to be acceptable. We sought to avoid rather than own and confront them.

Watching over the years my own and others' suffering in this process, I came to realize that it does not necessarily have to be this way – that by being conscious of ourselves we do not necessarily make life easier, but through understanding ourselves we can learn the lesson and move on, instead of repeating the same situation over and over again.

Boredom is fertile ground for observation; when I worked in the corporate sector, I was involved in any number of *bored* meetings. In an attempt to make life a little more interesting, I began watching my colleagues as they sat around the large boardroom table. By identifying their habits and using knowledge of what they revealed, I came to understand a lot more about them than I had before. This made it easier for me to work with them.

Endnotes

[1] It has been estimated that 0.3–2% of a paediatric population has OCD and 3% of adults have OCD. From Tourette Syndrome 'Plus' OCD by Leslie Packer PhD www.tourettesyndrome.net_overview2.htm

[2] Studies have also found that it takes an average of 17 years from the time OCD begins for people to obtain appropriate treatment. From OCD Foundation inc. PO Box 70, Milford, Connecticut 06460-0070 USA. http://www.ocdfoundation.org. OCD Information Centre 2711 Allen Boulevard, Middleton, Wisconsin 53562 USA.

[3] In 1999, Gail Steketee and her colleagues published the first long-term study on OCD. They followed 100 patients diagnosed with OCD for a 5-year period. Approximately 20% of the patients in their study had a full remission of their OCD and another 50% were reported to have partial remission at follow-up. Soke and Soke (1999) provided a 40-year follow-up on OCD patients. They reported that over 80% of all patients experienced improvement, including partial recovery with sub-clinical symptoms (28%), or complete recovery (20%). www.tourettesyndrome.net/ocd_overview3.htm.

Chapter Four
Healing your habits

Can you change your habits?

Our thoughts and actions create 'pathways' in our brains, like creating a new path in the countryside. As you walk the path each day, you trample down the bushes, squash the grass and push aside any branches. In time, the path starts becoming wider and more established. Just so, each time we respond to a situation in the same way as previously, we create a more established 'mind path'. As we repeat the thinking and response, so the pathway becomes a 'tarred road' and, in time, 'highways' develop, along which our responses travel. This means that, whenever we are required to respond to a certain type of thought or situation, our brains follow the road most travelled. Habits are no different, which is why it is so hard to let go of them. We have to train ourselves to turn off the freeway and start a new path, which involves change and hard work. The trouble is that when a crisis arises, we inevitably rush back to the old familiar path or way of doing things.

It might take less of an effort to stop smoking while taking a country break but get back to the office, where things are going badly wrong, and the need to smoke can be overwhelming. New Year's Eve is the time when many of us decide to rectify certain bad habits, but few of us maintain these resolutions for longer than it takes to cure our champagne hangover.

It is said that if you can maintain a cessation of your behaviour for 21 days (in the case of non-physical addictions) then you are a long way down the road towards maintaining the new behaviour. After 120 days you have truly turned the new path into an established road and are far less likely to revert back to the old road during periods of stress.

Why we find it hard to stop a habit

When change forces us to alter our lifestyle – for example, when we get divorced or are made redundant – we may have very little say in the process. What makes giving up habitual behaviour hard is that we have to engage voluntarily in the change. Now, change is not something that we humans tend to embrace: rather, we normally use up huge amounts of energy trying to ensure that change does not happen to us. So, when required to change a habit, we need a huge amount of determination and courage if we are to succeed.

Through achieving success, we add to our sense of self-worth, which gives us greater potential for further changes to be made. What we often do, though, is set a huge task such as 'I will stop eating chocolate, cut out alcohol and be sweet to my sister-in-law forever.' Yet the very next day we find ourselves retaliating snidely to our sister-in-law over a comment about our bulging waistline, while eating a slab of almond chocolate and feeling miserable about our puny self-control, all of which we have to drown in one too many glasses of Pinot Noir.

This erodes our self-esteem, which makes it harder to be disciplined the next time we decide to end a habit. The way to approach the issue, then, is with small steps which we *can* fulfil. For instance, in the case above, if we just made the aim not to eat chocolate for a day, then the goal would feel more attainable. At the end of the day we would feel good about ourselves and resolve to continue the process for another day, and so on. After 21 days the craving would have reduced and we could look at weekly targets, rather than daily ones. Now, having built on our success and affirmed a positive sense of self, we would be ready to handle the alcohol issue with confidence.

It's like throwing a small pebble into a pond and watching how the ripples increase in size as they move outwards. One small success can lead to far bigger ones. We learnt in school that nature abhors a vacuum, and this is also true for ourselves. When you get rid of a negative way of behaving, you create a vacuum which can be filled with a positive experience or behaviour. By overcoming your nail-biting habit, you have created a greater sense of self-worth and the gap left by the biting will be filled by something else. For every action there is a reaction, and stopping a habit creates some kind of ripple reaction in the world around and inside of you.

We have habits because they make us feel good. No matter how harmful they may be, they ease our tension and bring relief and release. So it's understandable that we would really not want to let go of something that gives us a reward. Someone who self-harms knows that what they are doing will cause a scar; the negative implications of this are surpassed by the emotional release.

Why change your behaviour at all? Why not continue to snore, be late, eat too much, grind your teeth, drink copious mugs of coffee whilst scratching your eye-brows and biting your nails? You've done it for so long and you're still around! Why waste the effort? There was a man you knew who had worse habits and he lived until 97! So why the need for change?

There is the change that is forced upon you, such as an accident or redundancy, but why would you volunteer to change anything that is not forced upon you? Because change is equivalent to growth.

Change is how we grow

If you examine old fossils of cockroaches, you will find that very little has changed in them over millions of years. Why? Simply because the cockroach has no known predators and so life has been relatively easy. It has not had to adapt or die, hence the lack of development. The more change you have had to face in your life, the greater the potential learning for you. This is how we grow emotionally and mentally: not when all is well and going smoothly. Who would want to change then? Hardship, then, acts as a stimulus for personal growth. Actively embracing change through your desire to stop doing what is keeping you stuck, is taking a courageous step to grow yourself.

Today we are confronted with change perhaps more so than any previous society. It's reflected in the clothes that we buy and trash months later when they are out of fashion, the appliances that seldom last longer than a few years, and the relationships that we fall in and out of more quickly than receiving our big burger and fries takeaway order. In times gone by, a suit was for life, equipment was made with skill and was repaired time and again and relationships lasted a lifetime. No more. Change has become part of our society, yet we resist it at every turn and, as it impacts more heavily on us, we become more stressed and act this out in detrimental ways.

Yet when we actively become the change – when we embrace it – we work with, rather than against, the process. A simple change such as drinking herbal tea as opposed to coffee can have a profound effect on our lives. Habits give us an opportunity to alter something, no matter how small, which creates the potential for many other positive changes to occur.

Take the example of a woman I worked with some years ago. Catherine saw herself as the classic victim. Her husband had left her for another, older woman. He provided little financial support and she was for the most part the sole provider for her two sons. Consequently, she worked ludicrously long hours and, feeling as if the world was out to get her, received just that sort of poor treatment from her clients. She felt hard done by her husband, her clients, his new wife, the children, her friends, the system, her life ... the list was endless.

One day she decided she simply had to do something to break out of this mould and so she began to learn Reiki, a healing system of bringing the body into balance. Suddenly she discovered she did have some power in the world – she could change the way other people felt, simply by putting her hands on them. Her confidence grew and she started reading and exploring further. Consequently, she no longer felt as if she were martyring her happiness for the sake of her children, but started looking for the aspects of her life that were really good.

She made the decision to sell a property and to use the money so she could cut down on the long hours she worked. The first clients to be fired were the unreasonably demanding ones. She moved the children to a good school close by, which was less expensive and involved less travelling than the more established schools that were farther away. The changes she implemented continued until she met a wonderful man. Within months they were married and she now has a loving relationship and lives in the country in a stunning house, where her sons have their own horses – a fairytale ending to a story that might never have been so, had she not taken the first step towards finding a way out of feeling that she was powerless to change her life.

In an art workshop that I ran, one participant had drawn her fists clenched in anger. She was very keen to find a partner, yet the fists being so closed showed that she was not ready and willing to receive someone else in her life. Her anger had closed her up. When she realized what she was subconsciously doing, she could make the emotional changes that would release the anger and so open up to the new. She has now found a wonderful, loving partner.

Change is like that. A little effort can have a profound, long-term effect. By identifying our triggers, we can start the process of creating a new life.

Your triggers and how to identify them

Triggers are the precursors to our performing our habits. We get anxious, so we suck the end of our pen. We are stressed, so we have another cup of coffee. We repress our anger and so indulge in a nail-biting session. Understanding what leads up to performing our habit can help us recognize the warning signs and so take preventative, alternative action. What we have to do then is discover other ways of releasing the emotions that trigger off the habit. We then find relief in a non-harmful manner. Here we look at how to go about doing this. Write your answers on a sheet of paper:

1. **Take a habit or behavioural pattern that you have and write it down, together with the goal that you would like to achieve. Set a time limit for this.** For instance, Samantha is always arriving late. Her goal is to arrive on time for the following week's appointments.

2. **Review the last three times you exhibited this behaviour.** Taking Samantha's example above, it involved being late to make a presentation for a client, being twenty minutes late for lunch with her friend, and half an hour late for a dentist's appointment.

3. **How did you feel emotionally, before performing the habit?** Samantha was nervous about seeing the new client, did not really want to meet her friend (as it was a lovely day and she wanted to be on the beach), and did not mind about being late for the dentist, as he often kept her waiting.

4. **How did you feel physically?** Samantha said that she felt tired, as she had stayed awake late at night working on her presentation.

5. **How did the habit make you feel afterwards?** Being late made Samantha feel angry with herself and guilty/apologetic.

6. **Is there a pattern?** Samantha's pattern, as she saw it, was that each instance involved doing things that she did not want to do. Rather than examine honestly what she could do to remove the 'shoulds' in her life and replace them with things she wanted to do, Samantha resisted the process by being late. Her lateness was a passive reaction to situations where she felt resentful for not being able to exercise free will.

7. **How do other people respond?** In Samantha's case, with anger or annoyance. This really mirrored her own anger at doing what she did not want to do.

8. **What is the outcome of performing your habit?** Samantha felt guilty for being late, but it did allow a sense of satisfaction in that she felt that she was not being totally controlled by other people. In a sense, then, it empowered her. This was why she repeated the behaviour, as it gave her control when she lacked the power to draw up her own set of boundaries. Had she felt empowered, she could have:

- Called up her friend to re-schedule or invite her to the beach.

- Mentioned to the dentist on her previous visit that she often waited up to an hour to be seen and ask him to call her if he was running this late so that she would not waste time.

- Examined what it was about her presentation that made her fear its rejection.

9. **What is it, then, that triggers your behaviour?** In Samantha's case it was doing what she did not want to do. She can now look at the week's appointments, see which ones she has an issue with and look at working with this; she does not have to respond by arriving late.

Using these nine questions, let's look at another behaviour and source its trigger.

The habit: Gail prides herself on the cleanliness of her home, to the point where she often wipes surfaces as much as ten times, even though she knows they are actually clean. 'I just want to make sure that no-one finds any dirt,' she says.

1. **Take a habit or behavioural pattern that you have and write it down, together with the goal you would like to achieve. Set a time limit for this.** 'My wasting time cleaning more than necessary – once per surface. I would like to stop doing this for a week at first.'

2. **Review the last three times you exhibited this behaviour.** 'When I look back on it, the worst times are after Harry, my husband, and I have had a fight.'

3. **How did you feel emotionally, before performing the habit?** 'I was upset at the things he had said to me. I felt worthless, so I lost myself in cleaning. At least that I could do.'

4. **How did you feel physically?** 'Not great. Exhausted really.'

5. **How did the habit make you feel afterwards?** 'Pleased that the surfaces were so clean. At least I could do something, even though I know I went over the top and wasted time.'

6. **Is there a pattern?** 'I had not thought about it before, really, but it does seem worse when I am upset about something, which is usually to do with my marriage. When things are going well I seem to clean but certainly don't re-clean.'

7. **How do other people respond?** 'Harry doesn't notice either way really, although he has made cutting comments about my sanity when I do it and he is around.'

8. **What is the outcome of performing your habit?** 'Satisfied. I can't really explain it any other way. Just good that things look sparkling clean.'

9. **What is it, then, that triggers your behaviour?** 'If I think about it, it's feeling a lack of self-worth, but also wanting to smooth things over – to make everything appear to be all right, even when it's not. I guess it's a way of avoiding facing how unhappy I really am in my marriage. I suppose I need to examine the emotional "dirt" in my life that through cleaning I am trying to eliminate.'

Through this process, Gail could start to become aware of what triggered her cleaning bouts and start to work with her marital problems and the effect that they were having on her family. She realized that she could not simply sweep this emotional dirt under the carpet.

Having gained insight into what really triggers your behaviour, you need to look at ways in which you can work with this insight in order to stop doing what you do.

Hindering your habits: methods of stopping

Many people have different methods for stopping habits, some of which work better with certain behaviours and personalities. I recall chatting to a woman who said that she had been a seriously bad nail-biter, until she became a nurse and had to change dressings, attend to bed-pans, etc. Suddenly, she said, the idea of biting her nails became less appealing when she remembered what her hands had touched! So, perhaps, like the nurse, you will fall into your solution by error; however, for most of us it takes much more effort if we are to succeed in stopping our negative behaviour.

Substitution

As the name implies, you substitute your behaviour with a less harmful practice. For instance, you can't stop snacking on chocolate and you've now acknowledged that the trigger is feeling uncared for: before the urge occurs, you have made the decision to substitute chocolate for fresh fruit, which you have made sure is handy, (not still sitting in the grocer's shop together with the chocolate bars!) Perhaps you could try a substitution that doesn't involve eating – such as having a long glass of water every time the craving occurs and saving the money you would have spent on chocolate, for the day when you can buy a luxury you really want.

Another suggestion for substitution is to keep a tally of each time you resist the urge, so that you can affirm your success to yourself. Each victory, no matter how small, affirms the one to come. This substitution method works very well for most physical cravings. (Obviously, substituting vodka for gin is not beneficial!)

Increasing your habit

WARNING: *This method is obviously not to be used for alcohol, drugs, by diabetics, self-harmers, shop-lifters, sex offenders and any other potentially harmful act or substance.*

When we constantly tell ourselves to stop doing something or do it less often, we create a greater desire to do the behaviour. Remember when your mum told you not to touch something and it became the very thing you desired to touch above all else? When we are not dieting, we seldom think of food when we aren't hungry. On a diet, however, it can become an obsession – waiting for the hour when we can have the recommended snack, longing for all manner of decadent foods and pondering how many more kilojoules a glass of wine has compared to the prescribed rice cake.

Giving yourself permission to indulge in the habit can very often be a way of limiting the obsession. If you normally eat two chocolate bars a day, go and buy ten and scoff the lot – by the fifth one you may feel like never wanting to eat another chocolate bar in your life. Precisely the thought you want. If you need to wipe the kitchen counter at least five times, adding on a further ten will create a situation where you start to experience dislike of the task and can see the absurdity in what you do. The same could be said for going back more than once to check that the car/house is locked. Make a point of checking at least five times each time you go out. In time, you'll get to the point when you will have faith that once is enough.

What happens here is that by allowing yourself to indulge in your behaviour, you remove that authoritarian voice within that criticizes you. You can't beat yourself up for something you've agreed to allow yourself to do, so the need often diminishes.

While you are over-indulging, be focused on what is happening to you emotionally. Do you go from feeling relief to anger and then to feeling foolish? Perhaps your emotions are different. Write them down – keep track of what is happening. The ego hates being exposed, and what you are doing is highlighting its struggle for domination within you. Confronting yourself like this is a courageous yet wonderful way of getting in touch with who you really are and releasing old patterns of behaviour.

Interruption

Our negative behaviour often occurs unconsciously. We idly bite the end of a pen, tap our leg or chew our hair, without even realizing that we are doing so. Once we have become aware of what it is we do and what triggers the behaviour, rather than berate ourselves, we can decide on another action to take, before we do whatever habit it is we want to indulge in.

For instance, if you often find yourself having too many glasses of wine during an evening out, make a rule of having a long glass of water between each glass. It's healthy and you'll feel better the next day. If you lose your temper easily, when you want to get out of the car and punch the fellow in front for taking your parking space, remember the discipline you previously planned, such as taking ten deep breaths and asking yourself if this act is worth losing your temper for. If you're inclined to gulp your food too quickly, then agree with yourself to chew each mouthful at least fifteen times and stop eating for two minutes altogether during the meal, three times.

Such interruptions not only make us more aware of when we are acting in a particular manner, but by the time we have done them, they often also alleviate our need to act in that way altogether. By the time you've drunk the water, you may not need the coffee any more. By stopping to ask yourself, each time you find yourself drumming your fingers, what you are feeling impatient about and then doing the pre-determined three minutes of drumming with your other hand before you can continue with your original hand, your need may have disappeared altogether.

Affirmations and goal setting

Many studies have been done on the effectiveness of actually writing down the goals you would like to achieve and creating a step-by-step path to them, as opposed to simply thinking about them. Goal-setting for your behaviour is a wonderful way of affirming your progress as well as honestly identifying your downfalls. The key is not to focus on those days when things went wrong, rather to affirm those days you stuck with the plan. Affirmations are a wonderful way of enhancing the process. By actually repeating the phrase you have decided upon, you make it more of a reality.

Let's take nail-biting. Having understood that anger and resentment are its cause, you can affirm 'I am able to release my anger,' or 'I let go of negative emotions,' or 'I am able to communicate how I feel to others.' Remember, though, to make the affirmations positive and make sure that they are spoken in the present tense, as if the desired behaviour has already been achieved.

Section Two

Examining Actual Habits

Chapter Five
The breath of life

Habits that affect our lungs and respiratory system

Have you ever considered that breathing is the only function in the body, apart from opening and closing our eyelids, which we can perform consciously or unconsciously? When we are relaxed and asleep, our breathing continues unabated, but we can choose to stop breathing, and hold our breath if, say, we want to dive under water. If we try to consciously accelerate or stop the heart or liver from functioning we would not succeed. The unique functioning of the lungs, being both conscious and subconscious, is why breathing is such an integral part of many spiritual practices, as a means to make the unconscious known.

Caroline Shola Arewa, author of *Opening to Spirit,* says: *The root word for* inspire, expire *and* spirit *and* respiration *is the Latin word* spiritus. *Thus we see that the breath and spirit are linked. In the yogic system, breathing exercises are called* pranayama; prana *means vital energy,* yama *means control. Therefore in yoga, to breathe is to control the vital energy…It is of particular importance to healers, shamans and those of us who wish to develop our connection with spirit.*[1]

If we have no spirit or soul, there is little point to our existence. We are spiritually dead while, if we have no breath, we are physically dead. Therefore, both are essential to our existence and it is surely no coincidence that their meanings interlink.

Spirits, in the sense of 'mine's a gin and tonic, thanks', came about through early alchemists, who saw the process of distilling crude fruit juice to a potent, strong and clear distilled form, to mirror man's spiritual growth, from rawness to great power and clarity. (I don't think they foresaw how popular the process would become and that drinking spirits would lead us not closer to but further from our divine selves!)

Breathing is both the first and the last thing we do when we enter and exit our earthly existence. When we breathe in, we absorb life-giving potential in the form of oxygen. When we breathe out, we get rid of toxic carbon dioxide. Were the process to be reversed our bodies would not cope and we would die within minutes. The rhythm created by inhaling and exhaling reflects not only how we live our lives, but also the rhythm of the universe. These opposite poles of tension, as we breathe in, and relaxation, as we breathe out, are used in spiritual breathing practices, to take us to a deeper alpha state of relaxation. Here, breathing symbolizes **duality**, in the form of tension and relaxation.

Breathing connects us to the world around us. The surface area of the lungs is far greater than that of the skin, and so provides us with a larger receptor for the outside world. We cannot *not* breathe. Even if the air is foul or polluted by our fellow human beings, we are forced to integrate with it, as is every other being. Breathing then mirrors our coexistence. No matter how much we may want to be insular, breathing reminds us that we can't be. Whereas we can move away from someone whom we would rather did not touch us, we still have to breathe in the same air that they do and in this way our connection becomes more intimate than the touch of skin.

Even plants assist the process by creating life-giving oxygen during the day and giving off carbon dioxide at night. As such the forests and flora represent the earth's lungs. (If only we did not spend so much time forcing them to smoke!) So breathing also concerns **interconnection** and relationships to other living things.

Breathing also relates to **boundaries.** If we feel smothered, and our independence is restricted, we may develop an illness such as asthma, where we battle to breathe on our own. Because at birth the closest relationship we have is usually to our mother, asthma can relate to a conflict between wanting to breathe independently of mum and yet fearing to do so. We don't have *room to breathe.* Others *take our breath away,* and we become dependent on medication to survive. We may want independence, but it scares us and we don't know where the boundary between the other person and ourselves begins or ends. As we get past our childhood years and become more independent, our asthma can disappear as we learn to breathe more freely.

Boundaries are established between the ages of six to 24 months, when a child first starts to learn that it is a separate being from its mother. This is the age when we learn to crawl and walk and when speech starts to develop. It is also the start of the 'terrible twos', when we develop will and control. It is not surprising, then, that asthma in children begins at around two to three years of age. If we experience too much restriction, such as very severe boundaries (frequent use of playpens, for example), excessive emotional control, limited movement, or the opposite – such as complete freedom in the form of neglect, denial of feelings and rejection – we will battle to sense where our control by others begins and our domination of them ends.

The more able we are to breathe life in deeply, the more willing we are to embrace life. Short, shallow breaths reflect a resistance to being fully in the now and absorbing every moment and bit of life-giving energy. We don't really want to take in what is happening to us.

Our inhalation represents how we breathe in life or take in the world around us. If it is fast, shallow and hurried, we are not fully absorbing all that life has to offer. How we breathe, then, becomes a mirror for how we are living our lives; habits relating to our breathing can give us a unique insight into where we have problems, of which we may not be consciously aware.

To **summarize:** habits related to breathing will concern issues of duality, particularly in the form of independence and dependence; absorbing the present or letting go of the past; communication and disassociation; spiritual progression or regression; relaxation and tension/stress; absorbing or rejecting; giving or taking; expressing or repressing; excessive or poor boundaries and restraint or freedom.

With that in mind, let's examine what's happening in people who make a habit of burping frequently.

Burping

In some cultures a good belch after dinner is considered to be the highest compliment you can pay to the host. In others, it could get you crossed off the guest list for good. While, strictly speaking, burping originates from the digestive system as opposed to the lungs, it nevertheless involves letting out (often foul) air. The odd burp, particularly after kippers or fizzy drinks, is common and an accepted part of the digestive process. However, there are people who make a habit of belching – most often young boys!

Because of its audibility and often offensive odour, belching is an act of aggression. It originates in the stomach, which in the Eastern Chakra system is associated with our warrior archetype. So, when we belch forth our fiery offensive gas, what erupts is an attempt to let present company become aware that we want to release some feelings of anger.

This often occurs at a time when we are extremely busy and there is too much happening for us to assimilate. Rather than swallow and digest the conflicting emotions, we seek to expel them. Our feeling of having no control over all this activity creates fear which we mask by aggressive behaviour.

By letting out air, we reduce the build-up of pressure inside the stomach, caused by undigested emotions (usually anger), which leads to heartburn. (The heart is emotionally burning with unresolved anger.) Rather than feel anger or aggression and deal appropriately with it (which would not be 'nice'), we swallow it, as in *swallow our anger*, where it *eats us up*. It may on occasion explode in a tirade, or simply simmer for years. Taking an antacid tablet results in burping, which brings relief to the acid/angry build-up which, like acid, has been eating away at us. As adults with heartburn, (too much fire in the heart) – which translates as thinking, as opposed to feeling our emotions – we often reach for an antacid tablet which results in burping, and the release of our frazzled emotions. Drinking lots of water can assist the problem, as the water reduces the acid build-up and symbolically flushes the issue out.

During Reiki sessions, I can often sense the pent-up emotion inside the client. It feels as if it is rising up through my body and is then expelled as a burp. In this act, which can occur frequently during the session, I can literally feel the client's body release tension and, in doing so, fall into a deeper state of relaxation.

Holding your breath

If we choose not to assimilate life, we hold our breath in the hope that life will stop, and we won't have to move-on. In most instances, though, holding our breath is a way of attempting to avoid an inevitable, unpleasant experience. When we are tense, we breathe short, shallow breaths as we don't want to assimilate what is happening. Fear causes us to stop breathing. Our body freezes, our pulse rate rises, adrenalin pumps and we go into a heightened state of awareness, holding on to our breath as if it may be our last. In a relaxed state, the opposite happens and we breathe deeply.

If you find yourself holding your breath and you aren't at the bottom of the swimming pool, it could be that you find yourself in situations that are causing you to live in constant fear. Ask yourself what or who you are afraid of. Is it worth not living your life for? Let go of your fear, breathe freely and deeply and enjoy this moment. Fearing the future lets precious moments of your life slide by unlived and prevents you from living you life to the full. Breathe in your spirit or courage, face the fear and move on.

Hyperventilating

It is estimated that 10% of the population has a habit of hyperventilating. This rapid but shallow breathing causes a loss of carbon dioxide and an increase in oxygen. The resulting imbalance causes pins and needles, dizziness, panic attacks, headaches, numbness and tingling sensations.

The original term for oxygen was *principe oxygene. Oxygene* comes from the Greek *oxus* meaning sharp or acid. Hyperventilating lowers the amount of carbon dioxide in the blood plasma, which makes us more acidic and less alkaline. (Oxygen increases the acidity in the body.) Acid/oxygen is a fiery, or masculine, principle – as in Genesis 2:7 when God is described as breathing life into Adam – while alkalinity is watery, or feminine. Drawing on the theme of duality discussed earlier in this chapter, inhaling can be said to be a masculine function, while exhaling is feminine. A diet of vegetables and fruit makes our systems more alkaline, whereas lots of meat – traditionally a more masculine diet – makes us more acidic. Dogs fed on alkaline diets are more passive, while those fed solely on meat become more aggressive.

When we hyperventilate, we are attempting to balance the masculine/feminine or fire/water energies within us. We have used up all the carbon dioxide/feminine energy which leaves us with a surplus of oxygen/masculine energy. In breathing as quickly as we can, we draw in more oxygen, or masculine energy, so that we can fight our battles with greater power. Shamans also use this technique as a way to enter an altered state of being, and primal warriors use a similar chanting and dancing to get into a trance-like, male energetic state before battle.

When we make a habit of hyperventilating, it is an indication that we often assume ourselves to be in 'fight or flight mode', where our security is in jeopardy. As in holding our breath, hyperventilating also relates to fear. The difference is that, whereas with holding our breath we seek to shut off life, in breathing very quickly we try to breathe in the fire that will enable us to defend ourselves. We panic and yet are afraid to change the situation in which we find ourselves. We fear the emotions that overwhelm us and attempt to balance our feelings with thoughts, because our feelings scare us.

If we are constantly finding ourselves in situations that make us afraid, it is an indication that we do not trust the process of life; rather, we have deep-rooted expectations that things will go wrong rather than right. Breathing in so much fire, we are eventually at risk of *burning ourselves out.*

We often worsen the effects of hyperventilating by smoking, which is another, more desperate, way of absorbing the fire we want and cutting ourselves off from our feelings.

Find the source of your fear. Are your masculine/feminine issues causing you grief or making you out of balance? Allow yourself a short time (ten minutes) every day to allow yourself to feel (as opposed to think) what it is you are afraid of. List whatever comes to mind, no matter how silly it may seem. Then, having given yourself permission to acknowledge these fears, start breathing deeply, until through the masculine and feminine principles of inhaling and exhaling you find yourself in balance.

Sighing

There are two types of people who habitually sigh – those who sigh on the in-breath and those who sigh on the out-breath. Usually, the former is a sign that we are stressed and the latter that we are relaxed. The in-breath sigh (often followed by a 'hmpfff' on the out-breath) is a way of letting everyone in the vicinity know that we are not happy, yet we are unable to put our feelings into words. The sound is universal in conveying our anger and stress at the situation. It is frustrating for those who have to listen to this simple but toxic message, particularly if it is repeated on a daily basis with no communication as to the real cause of the disgruntled sound. For the sighing person expects one to just know what the problem is. As such, this behaviour can be a manipulative and disempowered method of attack.

The remedy is to use sounds on the out-breath – such as 'harrrrrr,' 'haaaaaaa' or 'ahhhhhhh' – to release this tension and the anger that accompanies it.

Smoking

Smoking is more of an addiction than a habit, although it could be classified as both, for which reason, together with its exceptional popularity, I have included it here.

You remember earlier that I explained how breathing relates to duality – concerning aspects such as communication and disassociation;

spiritual progression or regression; relaxation and tension/stress; expressing or repressing; and restraint or freedom? Smoking is an attempt to balance these areas within ourselves. When we smoke, we draw in deep relaxing puffs of nicotine yet, when we crave nicotine, we get stressed again. The tar in the cigarettes fills our lungs, reducing the area of contact with the world outside. This demonstrates our fear of connecting to the real world, and we create a toxic barrier in order to avoid doing so.

When we desire freedom but feel restricted; when we want to be intimate and communicate with others, but are afraid to do so; when we are stressed and want be trouble-free; when we want to express our true feelings but are afraid to do so; and when we crave spiritual connection, but are afraid of the discipline and courage the step involves, we smoke to escape the reality of our lives.

Smoking is, after all, a habit of craving, and it is this craving, this attachment to the idea of how life should be rather than how it is, that has us reaching for another fag. That is the emotional reason why giving up smoking is so difficult. As well as the physical craving, not smoking involves dealing with how things are and not building smoke castles in the air when our dreams *go up in smoke.* Hit a crisis and the reformed smoker will desperately desire the escapism that smoking offers.

Often, cigarette-smoking is linked to drinking (most alcoholics are smokers). Because we are not balanced between our dualities, we drink to become more watery and then have to smoke to balance the water with fire.

Cigarette advertising (when it was still legal) showed images of how we would like our lives to be. For the grey man stuck on the same tube every boring day of his mundane life, the image of a macho, outdoor adventurer reflected to him the world he would like to inhabit. Likewise, for the rest of people scraping a living, the fun-loving, jet-setting, beautiful people became the goal they knew they had no hope of achieving. Still, smoking offered a way to imagine another lifestyle – to create a *smoke-screen* between how their lives were and how they could be. This lifestyle, smoking said, is just a puff away.

Smoking also affects our self-esteem. The yellow-stained fingers, the smelly breath and stained teeth, coupled with the knowledge that a simple leaf wrapped in paper has the power to make us tense, irritable and irrational when deprived of it, makes us feel disempowered. The numerous, failed attempts to give-up eat away at our sense of self, perhaps more so than any other habit, bar alcohol and drugs.

Fire is a symbol of transformation, yet the smoke of a cigarette is a cruel and mocking gesture of how stuck we are. We have *played with fire* and become caught in the nicotine trap. It takes only ten seconds from inhaling for nicotine to reach your brain. When it does, it releases chemicals associated with pleasure and concentration, and decreases the need for food as well as reducing stress and irritability. It's no wonder, then, that smoking is such a popular pastime and why, when the sensations are reversed due to withdrawal, you reach for another fag.

Many smokers start in their teenage years when they are feeling less sure of themselves. The world appears to hold so many riches and potential. Yet, although freedom is what they may desire, conformity in the shape of school is enforced; they have torrents of feelings with no way of expressing them, sexual urges abound yet often fill them with shame and confusion and they have no way of receiving the intimacy and acceptance they desire. In this confusion, smoking a cigarette becomes a way of smoothing the sharp edges of reality. It is a pattern which, commonly, will continue until their last (wheezy) breath.

Sneezing

We sneeze because something is irritating us. Often, we have an allergy to a particular substance that causes the problem, such as house dust-mites, cat fur, feathers or pollen. Therefore, regular sneezing and allergies are closely linked. Broadly speaking, allergies are expressions of subconscious, repressed aggression. The body regards whatever is breathed in as hostile and so expels it with force. The allergen may symbolize an irritating person or an uncomfortable situation which we fear and that we want to get rid of, and quickly! Fear always underlies aggression, and in 'fighting' the irritant, we hope to expel our subconscious fears.

The actual substance causing the reaction needs to be looked at if we are to find further clues regarding the area of our lives in which the irritant may lie. If it is cat fur, the issue may relate to a more primal or instinctive aspect of ourselves – or which we see reflected in another – relating to independence, femininity, warmth and intuition. Consequently, mother issues and independence from mother may be a cause. You may desire independence but fear leaving the warmth which mother represents, which causes frustration and irritation both with yourself and with her.

With dirt, or dust-mites, it may be a reaction to the dark side of life or ourselves. We don't want anyone to *dish up the dirt about us.* Feathers are thought to connect humanity with the Divine, hence the Native American feathered headdresses. If we are allergic to them, we may want to be a free spirit, able to soar to freedom, but find the idea of independence frightening. This issue of needing constant security may be our irritant. Pollen is the plant's 'sperm'. Consequently, an allergic reaction to pollen represents a fear of one's sexuality and fertility. It increases in spring, traditionally the time when mating takes place. With all of the above allergens, our reaction is to get rid of them quickly so that we won't have to experience what they represent.

Sneezing from allergens can also become subconsciously very manipulative, as loved pets have to be got rid of, rooms must be cleaned to absurd degrees, smoking is banned and special bedding purchased, in order for the sufferer to control the world they live in. Others are forced to comply; consequently, the sneezer gets to vent their aggression in a more socially-acceptable manner. This aggression is often born from a deep insecurity coupled with a desire for recognition or attention.

Old wives tales tell that wearing the actual allergen balances the allergic reaction in time and makes it impotent. This makes sense from the point of view that, rather than expelling it, the wearer is forced to confront the allergen and what it symbolizes. (However, this is not recommended without a doctor's advice.) It's a case of learning to love what one fears/hates. The more one gives power to the allergen, the greater its rule over everyone in the household will be.

In sneezing when we have a cold, we expel germs which become an attacking form of germ warfare! 'Come near me and you'll suffer the debilitating consequences of my attack.'

Sniffing

Unlike sneezing, when we sniff, rather than expel the issue, we try to hold it in. The watery fluid that we re-absorb is a mirror of the tears we have not shed. We are sad, but instead of letting the issue go, we hold onto it. The nose is also situated in the area associated with our intuition and the achievement of self-awareness. Perhaps by sniffing we are holding back on opening up to our intuitive self or intuition. Is there an insight or intuitive feeling that we are afraid to express?

By the audible noise we make, we want others to recognize our pain or the fact that we are not at ease. Do you feel you need attention, or for someone to pick up on what you are not able to express? We often sneeze and sniff at the same time. We get rid of our aggression (sneeze) and hold on to our sadness (sniff). We may feel we want others to help us, but are afraid to ask.

Years ago, my husband shared a flat with two other men. One was a quiet, shy man who often found it hard to voice his feelings to the six foot two, beer-swilling, rugby enthusiast who also shared the flat. Consequently, he sniffed constantly, which irritated both of his flatmates. He was often made fun of by his colleagues and did not have the courage to express the aggression he felt; instead he sniffed it in.

Another aspect of sniffing involves the actual nose itself. As with breathing in general, it relates to how we interact in life. One-day-old babies have been reported to indicate facial expressions that show dislike when subjected to foul smells, such as rotten egg. (Do not try this at home!) They also respond to the smell of their own mother[2]. We learn much about our environment, often subconsciously, from smell.

Smell is also an early-warning system, alerting us to fire or toxic chemicals long before the other sense organs would be aware of anything amiss. In a rather bizarre bit of research, women were found to be able to differentiate between the smell of sweat from the armpits of those watching sad or happy films.[3] We can therefore assume that many of our emotions are communicated through smell. We also know that those who have lost the sense of smell have a high rate of depression. Is this because they feel cut off from a deeper level of communication with others?

When we sniff, we may be intuitively picking up on another's emotions or *getting a whiff* of some aspect of a person or life that we don't want to take onboard and so we sniff disdainfully. We *look down our noses* at what is happening and yet feel, for whatever reason, unable to voice our disapproval. What is happening in your life that you don't want to acknowledge or recognize? Are you not receiving the recognition you deserve? Does this make you upset?

Snoring

Anyone who has lain awake at night while their partner snores will know just how tiresome snoring can be. It is estimated that approximately 40% of adults snore, with men far outweighing women in this habit.[4] (In the light of the emotional reasons for snoring, I will leave you come to come to your own conclusions!) It's not a great turn-on having your partner create a ruckus next to you, and this relatively small act has driven a wedge through many marriages, as the snorer gets dispatched from the marital bed.

So what causes snoring? Snoring occurs when the tissues and the soft palate lining the air passages vibrate. The tongue also falls back into the airway, narrowing or blocking it. This then forces air through a smaller passage more quickly, which causes the vibration. Anything that affects the weight, tension or size of the palate will affect snoring.

Being overweight will predispose someone to snore, because fat settles around the palate and alters its weight. Drinking alcohol and the use of sleep-inducing drugs will relax the palate muscles to the point of snoring. Having a cold, smoking, ageing, sinusitis, acid reflux and hormonal factors are some other causes of this annoying habit. The use of drugs that are inhaled through the nose, such as cocaine, will create inflammation in the area and increase snoring.

We snore on the in-breath which, as we now know, relates to the masculine principle and how we take in the world around us. When our bodies create a blockage that hinders this process, it indicates that we are not fully open to breathing in life's experiences, particularly in relation to male issues. We don't want to absorb what is happening and prefer to resist truly living. Snoring occurs typically at night whilst we are asleep, indicating that this blocking is a subconscious, sabotaging reaction. Consciously, we may feel we are open to change, but *sub*consciously our fear causes us to block it.

In sleep apnoea, we snore unevenly, usually building to an impressive crescendo, only to stop while we hold our breath and actually stop breathing. This can be dangerous and in some cases has lead to death. By doing this, we not only express our resistance to change, but indicate that we are almost prepared to die rather than accept it. (Like the groom-to-be who died of sleep apnoea the night before his wedding.)

Change becomes harder to deal with as we age, hence the increase in snoring as we grow older. Likewise, a smoker may be creating a *smoke-screen* between him/herself and what changes need to be made, while the person with acid reflux may be having problems digesting the new. Overweight snorers may be creating their *weight* in order to maintain a *waiting* situation so that they will not have to move forward. People who drink lots of alcohol and then snore show that they don't want to see the world as it is. When they drink, the idealized world they long for becomes possible. They drop their defences and the world becomes their friend. The world is a fiery, harsh place; dampening the fire with watery alcoholic drinks makes it feel better. Snoring then implies that they don't want to open up to the world as it really is. Nor do they want anyone else to burst their bubble.

When we have a cold, we often snore. This resistance to change is temporary, while we deal with our emotions – symbolized by the watery fluid which, like tears, is a way of shedding grief. With a cold, we are resistant to moving forward until we have let go of the grief of the past. We also like to hibernate in a warm bed and don't want to interact with others, thereby creating a safe space to work through the change.

Because of the guttural, harsh sound of snoring (which can sound like a growl or snarl) it can also indicate anger – both at ourselves, for not changing, or at others whom we see to be blocking our attempts to change. It also warns those who share our bed to back off and not to try to change us. (Smokers, drug takers and alcoholics are particular cases of those who would not welcome being told to change these addictions.) When loud, the noise is discordant and jarring, disturbing the normal rhythm of free breathing and the natural rhythm in our lives. Consequently, we can wake up feeling anxious and out of balance.

Many different methods exist to physically alleviate snoring; amongst them are moulded pillows, dental plates, sprays, tonics, plasters, vibrating wristbands and, in more extreme cases, surgery. What we really need to examine is where we are afraid to change. What is holding us back from changing? What area of our lives has become stagnant and needs a *breath of fresh air*? Are we really taking in and enjoying every breath we take? Find new ways to approach your life, whether it's as small as taking a different route to work, or doing something you've always wanted to but never found the time for. Then we can find new ways to breathe freely, absorbing each precious moment of our lives.

Sucking air in through closed lips

When we suck air in through pursed lips, we make a sound similar to the hissing of a snake. The resemblance to a snake is not co-incidental; our mood conveys that we are ready to strike out at anyone who crosses our path. By breathing this way, we limit and control the amount of the atmosphere around us that we absorb. The truth is, we don't want to interact with this world. We would rather suck back our venom, because we are afraid to breathe and voice freely how we feel. So we suck the toxic words in and bite our lips, hurting ourselves rather than the enemy. Through the hiss we let everyone know just how angry we are, and manipulate the situation so that it becomes controllable.

Endnotes

[1] Caroline Shola Arewa, p.83, *Opening to Spirit,* Thorsons, London, 1998.

[2] J.E. Steiner (1977) Facial expressions of the neonate infant indicating the hedonics of food-related stimuli. In *Taste and Development. The Genetics of Sweet Preferences,* J.M. Weiffenbach (ed.) NIH-DHEW, Bethesda, MD. J.E. Steiner (1979) Human facial expressions in response to taste and smell stimuli. In *Advances in Child Development vol. 13,* L.P. Lipsitt and H.W. Reese (eds.) Academic Press, New York.

[3] Ackerl, K., Atzmueller, M. and Grammer, K. *Neuroendocrinology Letters 23,* 78–84 (2002). Female subjects wore underarm (axillary) pads whilst watching a scary or a 'neutral' movie. The pads were then presented to a panel of women who were able to discriminate between 'fear' and 'non-fear' axillary pads.

[4] Snoring affects about half of men and 25% of women – most age 40 or older. From MayoClinic.com

Chapter Six
Chew on this

Behaviour that involves the mouth, biting and chewing

The mouth in general

We speak and breathe through it, use it for sex, eat and drink with it, and use it to blow bubbles! As such, the mouth truly multi-tasks, more so than any other orifice in the body. (It must surely be female!)

The mouth is the transition point for the outer world to become immersed with our inner world. Through speech, our thoughts are brought to the attention of those around us. By eating and drinking, we take in nurturing from the world. With breathing, we are uniquely connected to the outer environment, as we inhale the same air that friend and foe alike have breathed.

Functions of the mouth involve taking something from the outside world, digesting it internally and then expelling it. With eating and drinking, the food or liquid is eaten or drunk and the waste products excreted. When we breathe, oxygen is absorbed and carbon dioxide released. When we communicate, we take in mentally what we find admissible and express what we have gathered from the communication. Any emotional hindrance to this process will reveal itself through the mouth, either through what and how we eat, our rate of breathing or whether we speak or remain mute. Likewise, any behaviour that involves the mouth will reflect back to us issues relating to how we absorb or reject the outside world.

The other orifices in the body have less diverse tasks: the vagina has a sexual and birthing function; the ears are used for communication; the nose for smelling and breathing, while the mouth is the most important interface because it can be involved not only in most of these functions, but in others as well.

Whenever we have an imbalance related to what enters and exits from our mouths, it is an indication that we are hungering or starving for something. If the imbalance is breath-related, it's to do with independence; food-related imbalances express a need for love, nurturing or acceptance. A communication-related imbalance, may concern intimacy or truth.

Biting

In my first book on habits, *Healing Habits,* I did not differentiate between biting and chewing. On further reflection, however, I have come to understand that there is a subtle difference between the two. Behaviour involving biting is much harsher and more aggressive (as in '*biting someone's head off*') as opposed to chewing, which involves more a mulling over of concepts (as in '*chewing things over*'). Let's *get our teeth into* biting first of all!

When dogs are threatened, they bite. When contented, they chew a bone (or what they have just bitten – hopefully not the postman). Biting indicates a state of aggression where we will launch a *biting* attack if put under pressure. A humorous, but scathing, remark is described as having a *biting wit,* while an icy wind, that seems to eat through you, is described as a *biting wind.* Biting behaviour will do just that – cut your adversary to the core. Like an irritable Corgi, we may want to *snap* at someone but, instead, we muzzle ourselves. However, we live in a world where taking a chunk out of someone's backside because they jumped the queue at the deli is not socially acceptable. So, rather than *bare our teeth,* we have to pull our lips closed and conceal them.

Instead, we bite inanimate objects, such as pens, our nails, erasers etc. subconsciously wishing that our adversary was the object. We endure the situation and repress our aggression and anguish – as in *bite the bullet.* We might *bite our tongue* rather than express our anger, thereby harming and hurting ourselves, because we are afraid that by attacking we might *bite off more than we can chew.*

The different objects we choose to bite will indicate where our aggression lies. For instance, biting a pen may concern work-related issues. Do we need to put pen to paper over a particular matter but avoid doing so? If we bite an eraser, are we angry at not being able to *rub out*/eliminate an issue or person? (Fingernails are dealt with as a separate section later on in this chapter.)

The word bite originally came from the Indo-European root *bheid,* which means to split or crack. Could it be that we are afraid that by giving voice to our angry feelings, we may cause an irreversible crack or split in the relationship? Not being able to express our anger in a healthy manner pushes it into the realms of our shadow or hidden selves. Unable to harness our anger in a healthy manner, we might become syrupy sweet and exhibit passive aggression, or be prone to sudden, violent and abusive outbursts.

Chewing

When we chew things, as mentioned previously, we replace instant aggression with a situation that has been brewing for some time. We don't go out for the attack, as in biting, but rather break the issue down into digestible pieces. In the actual process of eating, biting comes first and only then do we grind or crush the food to make it easier to assimilate. Likewise, having accepted an issue we now have to break it up into emotionally-digestible bits. A resistance to chewing our food sufficiently relates to a desire to get rid of emotions that we find *hard to swallow*, which puts extra strain on our digestion. If you swallow too quickly without chewing sufficiently, what aggressive feelings do you find uncomfortable or difficult to digest?

Now let's examine more specific behaviour to do with biting and chewing:

Gum-chewing

Chewing, as in gum-chewing, can indicate that we don't want to digest and release an experience. We would rather go over it again and again. Perhaps through chewing, like a teething toddler, we soothe our fears and, through the sweetness, we create the illusion within ourselves that things are okay. Because we feel insecure, we allow the outside world in, but only to a controllable degree, and then we do not digest it.

Gum is flavoured and marketed to 'freshen the breath'. Maybe what we really need is to refresh our undigested, angry thoughts. Bad breath comes from deep, unexpressed resentment and anger. We have literally swallowed our festering feelings. By chewing flavoured gum we want to mask our toxic feelings and replace them with a 'minty freshness' that unfortunately, because the sweetness fades quickly, still leaves us with odorous thoughts. We often chew gum to appear cool and laid-back, masking our insecurity and repressed aggression. There is another reason gum is usually mint flavoured: anger falls under the element of fire. If we carry too much fire within us we will want to cool things down; what better way than with mint?

Eating too quickly and too much

People who eat quickly do not often give themselves sufficient time to work through issues and release them; they tend to rush from one thing to another, whereas slow eaters fully absorb all that an experience has to offer. Fast eaters may have any number of projects on the go at any given time, but may battle to complete them satisfactorily.

When we don't chew each mouthful sufficiently, we do not break the food down into small enough pieces to digest it efficiently. Swallowing food too quickly relates to a rush to take things onboard, but impatience with seeing them through. We also do not allow our appetite time to function properly and so often end up eating too much.

Guilt is another reason why we eat too quickly. When we feel bad about doing something, we tend to do it quickly and furtively. If we are already conscious about our eating habits, eating quickly may be a way of denying that we have eaten and a way to appease our guilt for having done so. As a child might gobble a stolen sweet, so eating quickly can be a way of getting rid of the evidence quickly.

If your companions are still toying with full plates while yours is spotless, ask yourself if you feel guilty about eating. Do you feel empty emotionally? Do you really crave intimacy and replace this need with food? What do you hunger for? What do you feel starved of? Are you seeking fulfilment with food when deep down it's your soul that needs replenishing? Eating should be a sensuous sensation, where we savour each mouthful, where we eat to enjoy not just to fill up. If we eat consciously, almost as a meditative practice, we will derive far greater pleasure from the experience and, by chewing our food a few more times, make it easier to assimilate – plus, it can assist weight loss!

Eating habits: craving particular food types

Sweet foods

When we cannot open a chocolate bar without finishing it, when we have to have at least three spoons of sugar in our tea, or when the cookie jar 'mysteriously' empties, we have to admit that sugar is an addiction. When we tuck into a large piece of gooey, chocolate cake, somehow life feels a bit sweeter.

Children are often given sweets in place of the love they need; it's a quick way to maintain peace. Consequently, children learn to replace their inner need for sweetness with an outer need for sweets. It's no coincidence that at supermarkets the checkouts have a great selection on hand. Just when mum is trying to unpack, the child will demand attention and, hey presto! a chocolate bar provides an instant solution. Any mother who has given in once will know that she has started a pattern which only enduring a hectic amount of temper tantrums will end.

Not being given sufficient love or nurturing leads to a deep-rooted anger, which is mirrored in our rotten teeth. We speak about having a 'sweet tooth', which is a sort of oxymoron as it combines that which is appealing and that which is repellent (sweetness and aggression). An overly-sweet person can become as cloying as a sticky toffee, and as hard to remove. Teeth represent decisiveness and aggression as well as boundaries. If we keep our mouth and teeth shut, nothing can penetrate us. Rotten teeth represent repressed aggression over decisions that have affected us, or boundaries that have been transgressed. The teeth which, in a primal state, we use to wound or attack become eroded, so our feelings erode us, creating pain and discomfort. The medical solution is to remove the decay and fill the hole with an impenetrable substance, or else to remove the offending tooth, which translates as removing what's emotionally eating away at us, and creating an artificial, impenetrable boundary.

Eastern Ayurvedic medicine relates sugar and milk to nurturing and mothering. As infants, we receive nurturing through our mouths in the form of breast milk. This is how we come to experience warmth and love. When we are not satisfied with sufficient nurturing as children, we will constantly seek to fill this empty hole with sweetness of a different kind. This can become a vicious circle as our hunger drives us to sweet foods, which create excess mucus and weight gain, which makes us feel less loveable and so less able to find love. We then attempt to sweeten our pain with more sweet foods and so the cycle continues. The word *sweetheart* aptly sums up the connection between sweets and the need for love. When in love, we can be said to be *sweet on* someone, which is another use of the word *sweet* that connects to the heart. When you long for attention or nurturing, do you *sweet-talk* yourself into having another choccy bar instead?

Look back to your childhood. Was your mother absent emotionally or physically? Were there too many other siblings fighting for her attention and love? Perhaps she was not nurtured herself and was consequently incapable of giving what she had not received.

Salty foods

Love crisps do you? Can't resist adding extra salt to your food before you have even tasted it? Salt, when taken to excess is associated with *cravings and compulsive desires* in Ayurvedic classification. When we have a craving for salty foods, we want to take in more fire energy, which relates to mental activities. It stands to reason, then, that a high intake of salt will be required when we need to pursue intellectual tasks or those that require thinking. This makes sense when we consider the vastly greater volumes of salt we are eating now as compared to previous centuries. We live in a world where male values dominate society, where more value is placed on thinking than on feeling.

In history, wars have been fought over salt, so highly were its attributes prized. The root word for salt is found in many other words, such as *sausage* (food made by preserving with salt), *sauce* (salty food), *salsa* and *salad* (meaning 'to put salt on'). The word *salary* comes from Roman times, when soldiers were often paid in salt, as in the phrase to be *worth your salt.*

Salt is also used as a medicine and preservative while, mystically, some people have used it to connect with the world of spirit. Salt is used to purify or cleanse and can destroy bacteria. Using salt heavily, then, may be a subconscious signal to cleanse and purify yourself of addictions or thought patterns, in order to bring yourself into balance.

Our blood tastes salty, hence Jews and Christians have used it in their ceremonies in place of blood. To say someone is the 'salt of the earth' implies in this context that they are the blood from the earth. As such, they are reliable and trustworthy – an attribute you would have when intellectual and emotional equilibrium has been attained.

Spicy foods

Another 'fire' food is spice. Ever wanted to *spice up* your love life? What is your *spice of life?* Want to *turn up the heat?* These are all phrases we commonly use to indicate that we want to make life a little more exciting. We've become tired of the bland and the routine. Add some spice to your food and life and you're seeking new thrills and excitement. Eating spicy foods is also about action and initiation. However, all this fiery raciness can be hard to digest and leave one gasping for water to *cool things down.*

Bland foods

Take away the sensuous spices, the richness of cream, the aroma of fresh herbs and you have a bland dish. People who are attracted to bland, flavourless food are afraid to embrace variety and the new. They don't want to add flavour and colour to their lives.

Often, arthritic and gout suffers and are put on a bland diet to reduce the acidity in their systems. Both illnesses relate to rigidity, control and perfectionism. These people may find it hard to digest experiences or foods that do not conform to their belief of how things ought to be. They need the blandness and the lack of spice to digest because it doesn't threaten them. They cannot tolerate the exotic and different and their bodies inflame and become painful when they have to digest this type of food. Sometimes, patients recovering after hospitalization or illness are required to eat bland foods, in order to give their bodies time to recover and digest the experience, before embracing the new thrills life has to offer.

Mushy foods

There are (believe it or not) people who love mushy foods such as mushy peas, mashed potato, porridge etc. Now, we all like a bit of this type of food, but when it's a dominant or exclusive choice and we aren't two years old, there's an emotional reason behind it. Many people with digestive disorders prefer this type of diet as it's understandably easier to digest. All the aggressive work of chewing and biting has already been done; they only need to swallow. Biting/chewing relates to aggression, as mentioned earlier, so such people can't confront their aggressive feelings. They want life to be soft and easy (don't we all!) as it was in childhood (mushy food is like baby food), where life can pass by without having to deal with issues, confrontations and challenges. It's all too much to cope with, which is why this diet is often used for the terminally ill. Mushy food is traditionally food that has been overcooked. All the nutrients and life-energy have long disappeared up in steam and cooking water. This also mirrors the mushy-food eaters' resistance to take in life-force and energy. It's simply too scary and too *hard to deal with*.

Tobacco chewing

The popularity of chewing tobacco has decreased. Nevertheless, if you do know someone who likes to chew tobacco, it may be of interest to know why they are doing so. For a start, tobacco, as we know, is highly addictive and results in a feeling of well-being – which is a pretty good combination in order for any habit to persist! By chewing tobacco, we attempt to calm ourselves and avoid digesting what has got us uptight in the first place. We then become addicted to creating the illusion within our psyche that all is well, rather than confront and release the issue.

Nail-biting

This is certainly one of the most 'popular' habits I have encountered: anyone from young children to adults bite their nails. Even though it is unsightly and sometimes painful when the nail-bed is affected, the biter seems compulsively driven to chew their nails. Breaking the habit is hard.

Another success was a friend who, having read my first book, was able to understand her emotional need to bite her nails and so address some of the issues. In doing so, the need to bite fell away.

In a primal context, our nails are used as weapons of attack or defence. When Cuddles the kitty puts her claws out, it's a sure sign that she means business and, if we are to avoid being scratched, we need to beat a hasty retreat. Our nails, like animals' claws, are related to aggression. We *have our claws out* when we are on the brink of attack. We speak of women who *claw their way to the top* of a corporation, meaning that they do so with determination and aggression, or who *get their claws into* an unsuspecting man. We *nail* someone when we get revenge, or seek to *scratch their eyes out*.

In a society where aggression is considered to be unacceptable, aggressive desires are suppressed. It just isn't on to claw the boss's face when you get overlooked for promotion. ('You scratch my back and I'll scratch yours,' however, works!) Consequently, we bite off the very weapons we would instinctively use to attack. We disarm ourselves and in so doing internalize our anger, where it eats away at us. We are afraid of our own natural, instinctive response and so destroy the weapons and *spit nails*. One must remember that exploding in sudden tirades of anger is not a healthy way of expressing one's anger. Rather, it is the result of repression that sits at the opposite pole of caustic, yet sugary sweetness. Neither is in balance.

This impacts on us further as, unable to express ourselves honestly, our sense of self diminishes. We are afraid of revealing the true nature of ourselves in case it offends and this fear eats away at us (as do we). We become fearful and nervous when emotions arise which we feel others would find unacceptable, in case we lose control. Ask yourself, when the urge to bite arises, who or what is it that you really want to claw at?

Why is red the most common colour used for nail-polish and lipstick? More recently, there have been blues and silvers etc. introduced, but women primarily have red toenails, fingernails and lips. Red represents anger and sexuality. (As in *seeing red*, a *red flag to a bull* or a *red-light district*.) Women with long red nails have long been viewed as 'femme fatales' seductively luring men to their fates. 'Don't mess with us,' the nails signify, 'we're not afraid to use aggression to achieve our ends. You cannot walk over us.' Red lips mimic a stimulated vagina. In a world where aggression and sexuality are suppressed, such public displays of these two traits are feared, and thus often belittled by other women who fear their own aggressive and sexual natures. It's just not nice!

Children and animals express what their parents/owners repress. So children who bite their nails may either be demonstrating their own suppressed, aggressive natures or have adopted their parents' behaviour. The parents may also be very controlling, both of themselves and of their offspring. Consequently, when 'unacceptable' feelings arise in the child – such as sexuality, aggression or the desire to control – tension builds, with biting providing the release.

In a society where so much attention has been focused on bullying, children have little opportunity to react naturally and physically to the taunts of others. Much as they might want to get involved in a skirmish, the fear of what reaction they may receive from teachers and parents limits them. So they have no way of dealing with the anger they feel, except to internalize it.

Having parents lie to us is another reason we learn to repress our truth. Sometimes we hear our parents say 'Yes, honey sweetheart,' when what they want to say is 'You lousy shit, do it yourself', or 'No, I'm not upset or angry,' when in truth they would like to claw their partner's throat. Where there is a lack of truth in the family and children hear their parents saying one thing while meaning another, they pick up the inconsistency between what they hear and what they instinctively feel. In the resulting dishonesty and confusion, they then learn that suppression is the acceptable or expected way to behave when they are angry; instead of saying so or physically attacking, they bite off their own weapons.

Skin next to the nail – biting

As mentioned earlier, any behaviour to do with biting is an act of repressed aggression. When we bite our own flesh, it indicates that something is *eating us up* – that we would rather digest an issue than express it. As it's not the nails but the skin that we bite, we are not wanting to attack another person, but rather allowing some problem to *gnaw away* at us. We may feel incapable of *getting to grips* with the real issue and be unsure as to *how to handle it.* Instead, we back-off and let our guilt at whatever feelings we have allowed to arise be placated only when we harm ourselves. By causing ourselves pain, we hope to appease our guilt for feeling as we do. The more we get tense about the situation, the stronger our feelings become and the harder we chew to suppress them.

Sucking

Sucking is what a baby does to receive breast milk. Whenever sucking is involved, whether it's sucking sweets or clothing, it indicates a deep need to reconnect with the feelings of safety and security we experienced as a baby. When our mothers had no more milk, were absent or occupied, we were given a substitute nipple in the form of a dummy, often dipped in sweet gripe water. Later we may have substituted our thumb to create the illusion that mum was still around. What this object provides us with, then, is comfort and stress release. If, as adults, we still cannot resist sucking the end of a pen or some other object, we reveal a deep-rooted desire to calm ourselves and to feel less fearful and tense about a situation in which we find ourselves. However, as with the dummy in childhood, it remains a synthetic substitution for real nurturing, and a painful reminder of the lack of intimacy we are feeling.

Babies have no teeth and consequently no ability to attack. Their boundaries are nonexistent and, when really young, they have very limited opportunities or abilities to make decisions. Feeling helpless causes anxiety and insecurity, which sucking soothes. When we feel helplessness, or as if our boundaries are being invaded and our will negated, we will be drawn to sucking as a habit.

Sucking in air (aerophagy)

This unusual behaviour involves gulping in air. We talk about *into thin air,* as in terms of disappearing or being non-existent. When we give the appearance of gulping (eating as opposed to breathing) what really amounts to nothing, we indicate that we are happy to swallow something which doesn't actually exist. Consequently, we kid ourselves that we feel okay about a situation and pretend to digest it or take the blame on board. We become a windbag – filled with false expectations yet, in reality, very empty. All this gas we've absorbed then gets released in a subtly aggressive manner when we fart or burp, which causes a stink. It's a childish, deceptive, passive-aggressive reaction to a situation with which we don't feel empowered to cope.

Spitting

When we are *spitting mad,* we cough up phlegm and expel it with force, not dissimilar to a snake spitting venom. We literally spit out the issue rather than attempt to digest it. Phlegm sounds like flame and indeed the word derives from the Greek *phlegma* meaning 'inflammation' and *phlegein,* which translates as ' to burn'. We spit out that which has *fired us up* or made us annoyed.

Sinus sufferers have to spit up vast quantities of phlegm in the mornings when their sinuses drain. Sinusitis relates to irritation or annoyance at someone close to us or at ourselves. When the phlegm becomes yellow or greenish, it's an indication of how toxic and infected the situation has become. Many sportsmen are captured on TV spitting on the field. Perhaps an opponent has got the better of them or maybe they have missed an opportunity to score. Spitting then rids them of their own need to take onboard the situation and blame.

Teeth grinding

Ever woken up and felt your jaw to be sore, or had a dull headache or earache that disappears as the day wears on, had facial pain, sensitive teeth or flattened teeth tips? Chances are you may be grinding your teeth at night. Medically known as bruxism, teeth-grinding is most common during sleep. Not only can it cause the physical discomfort already mentioned but, by exerting thousands of kilos of pressure per square inch on the teeth surfaces it can, over a period of time, wear down the teeth and loosen them, cause gum reduction, chipped enamel and jaw joint problems as well as leading to fractures in your teeth. Yet you may be completely unaware that you are grinding.

Teeth-grinding has been attributed to stress and anxiety as well as sleep disorders and an abnormal bite or missing or skew teeth. Some studies have also shown that a lack of pantothenic acid (an anti-stress vitamin and a factor in motor activity control) may be a physical cause. A calcium deficiency, which can cause muscle cramps or involuntary movement of muscles in the mouth resulting in grinding, may also be a factor, while a parasitic infestation can also cause teeth-grinding. There has also been some recent evidence to show that selective serotonin re-uptake inhibitors, such as Prozac[1], can also increase tooth-grinding. Yet, as we know, nothing happens on the physical level without an initial emotional cause. The subtle (i.e. the mental/emotional) always affects the gross (physical) and not the other way around. So ,in spite of all these physically-contributing causes, we need to see what is happening in the subtle layers of our being.

People who teeth-grind have also been found to be more prone to biting their fingernails, pens etc. or the inside of their cheeks.

Like our nails, teeth are also a means of attack, as in *fighting tooth and nail* and *armed to the teeth.* They are also used as a means of grinding down food into more easily-digestible parts and can also represent decisions. Grinding our teeth is a way of blunting our attacking instruments. We grind our teeth at night, indicating that it is a more subconscious response to deep-seated aggression-related issues. These unconscious issues are the *daily grind,* which slowly wears us down. We feel impotent and lack the confidence to attack what troubles us and so we grind our teeth in an act of passive aggression. As this is a repeated behaviour, it indicates that the issue will not go away but continues, often for years, to be indigestible. The mouth represents a boundary, so the aggression may well have to do with a feeling that our boundaries have been threatened; someone has invaded or taken something from us – naturally, we desire revenge.

By grinding food down we allow it to pass through the digestive system easily. When we grind our teeth we do so not with food but with an emotion that we cannot swallow. No matter how many times we grind, we are still left with an empty mouth. So our efforts are worthless. We feel incapable of reducing the problem to *bite-sized chunks*. We fear the problem for which we cannot find a solution.

Teeth represent decisions because they form a strong boundary between what we allow into ourselves and what we exclude. By opening them or shutting them, we make decisions as to how to interact with the world. We decide what to include or exclude. When our teeth give problems, we may be having difficulty in taking decisive action or *getting our teeth into* something.

In summary, then, we may be feeling stressed and afraid about decisions we need to take involving issues that we feel angry about, but are unable to come to grips with. We may then seek revenge.

Vomiting and self-starvation

(See also Chapter Fourteen for discussion of self-harming.)

When we do not want *to stomach* something, we expel it. We can't hold it down or accept it. It can be an emotion, an experience, an aspect of ourselves or a person that we find *hard to digest*. The issue *makes us sick*. And when the body has something it finds disagreeable it expels it. However, we are more interested in the reasons behind the behaviour of those who force themselves to vomit, as in the case of eating disorders. Eating disorders affect women almost exclusively and can be very serious, with 20% of anorexia nervosa patients actually dying from their illness.

Anorexia nervosa and bulimia are very complex emotional illnesses and consequently beyond the scope of a few paragraphs in this book. Help from professional therapists and doctors is essential to recovery. Force-feeding seldom helps and more often drives the compulsion deeper. Eating disorders are born out of a desire for physical, and sometimes spiritual, perfection – greed versus asceticism in a seesaw of emotional behaviour. Bingeing reflects the one side and starvation the other. The resulting guilt is rectified by vomiting, which is kept hidden from others. It masks a huge desire for attention, which the sufferer veils by self-sacrifice.

There may have been a number of causes in childhood that brought on this cry for help – such as very strict, authoritarian parents; the role of the child and parent being reversed; one's will being nullified; and constantly being shamed. Shame is perhaps the greatest cause, for when we have been constantly told that what we are is not acceptable, we cannot develop a healthy sense of self-esteem. Being shameful, we are most shamed by our natural instincts, which we feel required to control. But natural instincts cannot be suppressed ad infinitum and so when they do emerge; they do so in a shadowy way. Where we have curtailed our eating habits with utmost discipline, we may resort to bingeing in an uncontrollable manner, for which we feel guilty and attempt to purge ourselves, which causes us more shame and so the cycle is perpetuated. By martyring ourselves through starvation, we attempt to appease our guilt.

Deception plays a strong role and, in many instances, family members may not be aware that there is a problem. The anorexic or bulimic person may exercise strenuously (though how they do so on so little food is a mystery!), enjoy cooking for others, and devise every clever method to dispose of uneaten food and disguise their weight loss with bulky clothing. Laxatives may be taken and, when they do eat publicly, the food might be really Spartan, such as undressed salads, bland, no-fat health foods etc. The desire to reject what nurtures them is often a desire to reject all that is feminine in its rounded, swollen, moist form. They desire to remove themselves from all that is physical in order to reach perfection. For how can something that bleeds, smells and sweats be perfect? The sufferer's relationship to the body is such that they want to rise above it, to transmute it; death holds little fear, and in some cases may appear to be a comfortable release.

In rejecting what nourishes us, we are, in a sense, not wanting to digest the instinctual issues of life, yet desire them nonetheless. This is a serious habit and requires medical and psychological intervention.

Endnotes

[1] Teeth-grinding: www.health911.com/remedies/rem_teethg.htm

Chapter Seven
Do that to me one more time...

Sexual behaviour

Why do some men find a blow-up plastic doll more appealing than a real woman? Why would a powerful CEO voluntarily allow himself to be beaten and humiliated? And why do men enjoy phone sex? From cross-dressing, sadomasochism, fetishism, exhibitionism, obscene phone calls, incest and copulating with corpses, men have the upper hand. Why is this? (Research by Liam Hudson and Bernadine Jacot, the authors of *The Way Men Think,* states that in 99% of sexual aberration cases, the perpetrator is a man.[1])

There are any number of sexual deviations – including *xenophilia*, the sexual attraction to foreigners or aliens, (which gives a whole new twist to *'beam me up, Scotty'*), *plushophilia*, the sexual attraction to stuffed toys, and *harpaxophilia*, which is the sexual arousal from being robbed. We will only focus here on the more common types of paraphilia.

Given the attitude of many parents to sex, due to their own repressed shadow issues, much so-called 'extraordinary' sexual behaviour gets passed down from one generation to the next, simply because no one is telling. Sex becomes a shameful desire rather than a healthy, enjoyable one. In most sexual habits, shame which originated in childhood is the major contributor.

For example, let's imagine a young child playing happily with his or her penis or vagina, simply because it feels good. Mum steps into the room with a friend and, in her embarrassment, yells at the child to stop immediately. The child is made to feel ashamed for what was simply a natural, exploratory act. From now on, the child learns that it is 'bad' to touch him/herself and so must do it furtively, in fear of being caught. Later in life, the desire to play with him/herself publicly may be fuelled by the thrill associated from childhood experience. This is not to say that every child caught playing with him/herself will become a flasher, but the experiences of childhood do form the potential for what will emerge in our adult sexuality. Obviously, it's inappropriate to let our children masturbate at the dinner table, but we must not shame our children for doing what comes naturally and we need to handle the matter sensitively.

Any exploratory sexual behaviour which a child is made to feel is unacceptable and shameful will be suppressed and have the makings of sexual-shadow habits, which will emerge later in life, as do all repressed desires and urges. With so much ignorance and fear relating to what is our most powerful urge, it's understandable why so much shadow behaviour emerges through sex.

In a sense, we all have sexual pervasions of one kind or another, yet most of us curtail these desires so that we fall within the social norms of our society. If, however, we remove the influence of society (such as suggested in William Golding's novel, *Lord of the Flies*), this structure breaks down very rapidly. This implies, then, that it is our fear of being ostracized that curtails our desires, rather than our not having them in the first place. The pervert, however, cannot, for reasons explored later, manage to suppress his urges and, once acted upon, a Pandora's Box is opened which can usually only be closed with extreme therapeutic intervention.

Many people claim not to dream. Why? Because often their dreams involve wild sexual happenings that are uncomfortable to their conscious minds. Take, for instance, the upstanding member of society who dreams of same-sex orgies with whips and leather outfits. The dreams are both disturbing and confusing. What better way to overcome the dilemma than to shut it out unconsciously?

Sexual gratification which is atypical and extreme goes under the broad heading of *paraphilia* and may be associated with either objects (as in fetishism), a particular act (as in sadomasochism), or a type of person or animal (such as a child for a paedophile). Once the fixation is ingrained it seldom changes and, often, gratification can only be achieved by using or fantasizing about the object, act or person.

The most common acts of paraphilia are: paedophilia, exhibitionism (exposing genitals to strangers), voyeurism (surreptitiously observing others having sex, urinating, etc.) and frottage (where the perpetrator rubs his penis against non-consenting individuals – popular in crowded tubes) and sexual phone calls. Fetishism, sadomasochism (being humiliated or made to endure pain), cross-dressing, necrophilia (sex with dead people), bestiality or animal sex, behaviour to do with elimination of faeces and urine -all are also not uncommon. Sadly, paedophilia is the most common form of paraphilia. Obviously, because much of this behaviour is forced upon another and threatens their free will, particularly in the case of children, it is illegal and **extremely psychologically damaging to the victim.** Help and intervention needs to sought from trained therapists, if others' lives are not to be irrevocably damaged.

Once their boundaries have been violated, without intervention they may fall prey to further violations, wreaking havoc later in life in relationships where trust and intimacy are required. Having been abused sexually, confusion develops between pain and pleasure and they may feel ashamed for feeling pleasure, or emotionally pained yet physically experience pleasure or restrict pleasure, so that painful memories won't emerge.

Now, before we all disappear into guilt, the difference between paraphilia and someone who enjoys, let's say, phone sex with their partner occasionally, having their partner dress up as a nurse, or watching the odd blue movie, is that this is not the only way he or she can achieve arousal or orgasm; whereas with paraphilia it normally is. In other words, in paraphilia, the behaviour is compulsive or has created a dependence.

Many theories exist as to why this behaviour might have developed. Perhaps one of the most common reasons is a problem with having close or one-on-one relationships. Lacking this intimacy, the paraphiliac reverts to a fantasy world, reverting to childhood sexual behaviour or conditioning. Often, then, the paraphiliac starts preferring (or finds that behaviour more stimulating than) conventional sex. Children who either observe or are the victims of paraphilia start imitating what they have experienced. Later in life when sexual gratification is required, it may be less threatening and more exciting to choose this learnt, but often socially-unacceptable, way of gratifying sexual urges.

We have inherited much of this social perversion from the Victorian era which, while having the highest ever proportion of prostitutes to population in England, was bound by strict and perverse moral doctrine. Child prostitutes were highly prized by many of the most upstanding members of a society that had become completely unbalanced. For instance, take the bizarre practice of Dr Kellogg, who promoted the practice of threading wire into a boy's foreskin to prevent him from getting an erection. Such aberrance was not uncommon and much of the perverse activity that abounds today has its origins in this era.

For the rest of us vanilla sex is on the cards!

Some of the more popular paraphilias are now explained in greater depth.

Anal sex

Anal sex is a fairly common form of sexual behaviour. It can be performed manually, orally or by anal intercourse, either as the primary form of sex or in addition to other sexual behaviour. Normally considered the domain of homosexuals, anal sex is also enjoyed by many heterosexual couples. Some men enjoy being given anal sex because it can stimulate the prostate, which gives extra pleasure when experiencing orgasm.

When we are babies, we learn sensuality/sexuality first through our mouths and then through our anus. As we grow, we move away from the anus and extend our exploration into other erogenous zones. However, to some extent, there is still a residue of anal desire in all of us. When you see an attractive young man or woman, what do you often look at? His or her buttocks. Why? Because the buttocks are the pathway to the anus. Like the lips of the mouth or the vagina, their large voluptuousness entices further exploration.

Because the anus was designed to expel as opposed to intake, the anal sphincter muscle tightens when stimulated and consequently the act can be painful unless the partner is patient in stimulating his/her partner.

The ultimate spiritual experience is one of divine ecstasy, ego-lessness, and the blissful realization of transcendent identity. In becoming one with another you mirror becoming one with God as in *unio mystico*. However, for most of us, it is often an act where the two polarities of ourselves (fire and water) attempt to achieve balance. Sex, in the Eastern Chakra energetic system resides in the second Chakra, which is also home to issues about money, boundaries, control, emotions, manipulation, relationships and our desire for external power, all of which may play a role in any sexual behaviour.

Just as in vanilla sex, in anal sex these issues can come into play. For one person it may be an act of surrender, while for another it may involve reinforcing or experiencing domination. It could therefore be that those who enjoy being in the penetrative position in anal sex may be drawn to it as an act of experiencing power over another person. (Primal warriors would rape their prisoners, not from lust, but as a way of humiliating their enemies.) Those who are receiving may be enjoying exploring the act of surrender and the paradoxical power that comes from being controlled by another yet, at the same time, because of the penetrator's desire, actually controlling the penetrator.

Cross-dressing

Cross-dressing, if you are unsure of the term, refers to men who dress in women's clothes. They are not transsexuals, who feel as if they are women trapped in a male body, neither are they drag queens, who dress up as women to entertain and pick holes in society's stereotypes or to entice same sex partners.

Most cross-dressers are ordinary men who simply enjoy the experience of exploring their feminine nature. Cross-dresses fall into no racial, religious or economic stereotype. Most are heterosexual and many are, or have been, married. They form an estimated 5% of the male population.[2] That's one in every twenty men you meet! Yet they still are largely shunned by society and often have to lead a double life, of which even their partners may be unaware. There *are* women cross-dressers; however, because it is acceptable for women to wear more male-orientated clothing, such as jeans etc, they can pass unnoticed in society, unlike a man in a mini skirt! Because of society's general intolerance of anything other than stereotypes, most cross-dressers live in fear that their secret will be discovered and that, should that happen, they will lose their jobs, families, friends and partners.

Trying to discard this behaviour out of fear or guilt is often unsuccessful; it is as if the man is denying the expression of an important aspect of who he is. Telling a partner may be very traumatic as to do so exposes one's most vulnerable nature. However, the relief at feeling accepted for who one is by one's partner is huge, not to mention the new level of honest communication that will have taken place. Constantly hiding a secret from a partner is not the ideal way to conduct a relationship, if true intimacy and integrity is the goal. From the partner's point of view, once the realization has been reached that their partner will not leave them, they can learn to accept and appreciate the relationship.

When to come out of his partner's closet and open up is something that each individual will have to ascertain for himself, based on his insight into his partner. The longer a cross-dresser waits to tell his partner, the more negative the reaction is likely to be. Perhaps seeing a qualified counsellor will help explain to the partner what has been shared, as well as answer any other questions.

Like most habits, an increase in stress will exacerbate the need to cross-dress. It is important for the partner of a cross-dresser to understand that no amount of coercing or threatening will in the long-term be able to stop the habit, even if the cross-dresser shows a desire to do so. In most cases, in time the desire will overcome the intention to stop – just as it does when asking a woman to stop shopping! Equally, you cannot force your partner to accept your role as a cross-dresser. They may need time to accept this new dimension of yourself. Sometimes a partner will feel they are to blame for the need to cross-dress – as if they weren't woman enough to maintain the illusion of what a relationship should be.

Once out in the open, boundaries will need to be discussed, in terms of what is and what is not acceptable. Who else (if anyone) to tell, whether the partner is prepared to join in the activities etc. all need to be mutually agreed upon.

We are all sexual creatures, and so naturally many cross-dressers find the experience sexually stimulating. Whether or not sexual stimulation or orgasm is part of the experience, the urge to dress in feminine clothing is strong, and without it the cross dresser would feel all the angst of a painter without paint.

The cross-dresser may, in order to fulfil his habit, spend huge amounts of money on clothing, make-up and accessories, which could impact on his family's needs. It may, as with many habits if unchecked, become so all-engrossing that he neglects both family and work commitments.

In most cases, having the need to cross-dress carries with it a degree of shame and guilt, both of which hinder us from achieving a high level of self-esteem. Consequently, we may feel unlovable, which could affect the type of relationships we choose to be in. Loneliness is also a factor, as the cross-dresser may at times feel that he is the only person in the world who has this habit. A society largely uneducated in the nature of cross-dressing may regard the cross-dresser as homosexual, a pervert or mentally ill. Fear of being accidentally discovered by a family member, and being outcast, is also a constant shadow that looms over the cross-dresser.

As discussed earlier, we all have fire and water elements, or male and female aspects. When a man has (usually through his upbringing) been made to deny or discard his feminine nature, it falls into the shadow aspect of himself, or closet out of which he emerges, transformed into a woman. In spite of the necessary clandestine nature of his secret, and the fear of discovery, dressing as a woman brings relaxation and a greater feeling of integration.

In many cases, the boy who becomes a cross-dresser has been shamed for displaying traits that his peers and family consider feminine. Consequently, he represses these traits in order to avoid further humiliation. He develops as a normal man and follows the ups and downs of marriage/relationships and career. Yet this unexplored aspect of himself begs to be explored, but at what cost? Confusion as to his sexuality combines with a strong urge to reintegrate his male and female sides, which is healthy and natural. Yet his means of doing so feels unnatural and he may experience guilt and a fear of being found out.

He may have inherited an idealized, macho view of how a man should act, which makes his desires all the more confusing, restrained and scary. For many years he may swing between his need to cross-dress and the guilt that tells him not to. This eats away at his self-esteem and he feels caught between his need to feel accepted by society and his need to fulfil his own desires.

In an ideal society, the cross-dresser would be allowed to explore his desire openly and non-judgmentally until the combination of his male and newly-acquired female persona results in a more mature and integrated personality.

On the positive side, finding out that your partner is a cross-dresser can provide you with a great boutique-shopping companion! Unlike when you go with your girlfriends, you can have great sex afterwards! The downside, of course, is that your man can end up looking better dressed and sexier than you!

Exhibitionism

When I attended an all girls' school we had an exhibitionist whom we called Wobbles. Wobbles (and I suspect there were a number of characters playing this part) would come and stand up against the wire fencing of the tennis courts and proceed to display his wares to a screeching bunch of girls, who would run away giggling wildly. All of which was precisely what Wobbles wanted. Because Wobbles, and so many other men like him, get aroused by causing shock to unwilling victims. They literally 'get off' on shocking behaviour, which no doubt relieves their tension. Stress exacerbates the desire and tension builds until they expose themselves again.

Whilst Wobbles, probably because of his distance from us and the power that comes with being in a pack, did not badly damage us psychologically, exhibitionists can cause huge damage to their unsuspecting victims, particularly if they are children and /or if masturbation takes place.

Few exhibitionists will rape[3], although some rapists are exhibitionists. In most cases no actual sexual contact is required; however, this is a serious offence and can lead to a prison sentence. Boys younger than 18 may be exhibitionists and the behaviour may continue throughout adulthood.

Female exhibitionists are fortunate in that most men would enjoy the sight of a naked woman flashing at them and would probably not report the experience. As a safer bet, many can seek employment in conventionally-accepted venues, such as strip-tease bars for instance, although it is not true that strip-tease dancers are necessarily exhibitionists.

Often, the victim's shocked reaction not only arouses sexual excitement, but also affirms the exhibitionist's masculinity. (Of course, nowadays you can just go to the Tate Modern and expose yourself in the name of Art *and* make money from doing so!)

It's advisable to seek treatment early on before the person gets into serious trouble. Many different approaches are employed, from the use of negative stimuli ('shame therapy') where the goal is simply to shame the offender into stopping, and the more compassionate approach of restructuring the distortions of thinking (such as the belief that the victim deserves to watch the exposure) and creating empathy for the victim.

Fetishism

The word 'fetish' comes from the Latin *facticius* which means 'made by art', as in manu*facture*, or made by man. Related to *facticius* are words such as *facio* (from which derive words relating to idols and idolatry) and *facturari* ('to bewitch'), which are used in the context of witchcraft. In the sixteenth century, Portuguese sailors discovered, on the West Coast of Africa, natives using objects which they had made for worship. These they called *feitiço*.[4] From this, the meaning diversified over the years to relate to any object used as an instrument of worship or containing a spirit. It is very closely linked to the supernatural and may be made from an assortment of herbs, material, stones, bones, wood etc. Voodoo and Odoism are instances of African fetishism transplanted to American soil, presumably from the days of the slave trade. Here they took on a more sinister meaning, as human sacrifices were not uncommon up until the late nineteenth century.

Sigmund Freud was the first to define sexual fetishism[5], although the act has existed for centuries. The term derives from the concept that, as with religious fetishism, an object has supernatural power over the participant, only now the power is of a sexual kind. His theory was that, when a boy first notices his mother's lack of a penis and diverts his eyes from her, the first object which he focuses on becomes the fetish object. The fact that women display fetishistic behaviour as well makes this theory highly improbable.

Fetish objects have no limits and can literally be any object, though more popular ones include shoes, boots, stockings, pants, hair, Lycra, furry animals, Latex, toes, legs, bras, negligees, gloves, rubber, leather or silk. More often than not, these objects must have been used or worn – not so much as a reminder of the previous owner, but more as an object in its own right. Objects carry the *od*, or vibration, of past experiences which is what makes them so attractive. Even if the object belongs to a close partner, sexually speaking any act involving the object will be depersonalized. The object develops its own emotional nature in the eyes of the fetishist, just as a Voodoo doll does to a voodoo practitioner. In time, the object becomes empowered by the amount of energy that is placed in it – much as a holistic healer's crystal or precious stone carries additional energy, as does a talisman that has been developed for a specific purpose.

There are two main types of fetishism: *form fetishism,* where the actual shape is important and *media fetishism,* where what the object is made of, rather than the object *per se* is important. Fetishists may decide to make a collection of the type of object they have chosen and may even steal to enhance it.

Masturbation or enhancing sexual activity is almost always what the fetishist seeks from the object. Often they can only reach orgasm if the object is part of the experience, or fantasized about during the act, or if the object is used in a certain manner by a partner. For instance, the partner might be required to wear the boots, or stroke the genitals with silk. Only in rare cases does the fetishist pose any danger to others and they usually pursue their activities in private. Their desire for the fetish object can range from a mild interest (which is common) to compulsive behaviour, which may be more problematic.

When a boy is required to withdraw from the intimacy of his maternal relationship, his primal source of comfort and nurturing is gone. If he resists the process, he cannot fully embrace his manhood. Yet, by *not* resisting it he is deprived of his closest, most intimate relationship With this trauma comes a feeling of loss, aloneness, anxiety and lack of intimacy. Most emotionally-stable boys are able to cope with this experience, but in some cases, where the boy is withdrawn, lacks self-esteem or the ability to relate to his peers (and particularly if he has had a traumatic exposure to sex) he finds this stage very traumatic and fetishism may provide an answer to his demanding sexual appetite. At the age of fourteen he is not sufficiently emotionally-developed to have an intimate relationship with a girl. Feeling estranged, it is easier to confuse people with objects and vice versa.

Objects are less threatening, don't reject, and are therefore easier to relate to, as he has complete control over them – as opposed to feeling a lack of control with another person. Impersonal becomes easier than personal; when it comes to relationships, studies reveal that fetishists have poorly-developed social skills and problems with establishing intimate relationships. Deprived of normal sexual contacts, the fetishist becomes more and more dependent on his object for gratification and further removed from intimacy. He may then create a persona around his fetish object, charging it emotionally whilst depersonalizing people.

Paedophilia

The word 'paedophilia' comes from the Greek words *pais (paid-),* meaning 'child' and *philos,* meaning 'loving'.

One of the distinguishing aspects of the paedophile is his (for the majority of paedophiles are men)[6] complete denial of his activities and delusional belief that his activities are, in some way, actually beneficial to the children he molests. Even if caught, tried and found guilty they will, in all but the rarest of cases, protest their innocence. More than is so with any other paraphilia or sexual perversion, the paedophile is and remains in complete denial. Not taking responsibility for his actions means that, unless caught, he will rarely admit to having a problem and seek help. Treating a paedophile also proves problematic as he does not recognize that he has a problem; therefore he does not feel that he needs treatment.

I personally have witnessed this on a number of occasions when counselling paedophiles on a call-in counselling service. They either use erroneous logic (such as 'she was dressing provocatively because she wanted to have sex with me') when referring to a minor, or lead themselves to believe that the victim was in some way deserving of the act and therefore a willing party to it. One young man, a sports coach, led a party of young boys to an overseas event, where he molested them. Even when confronted with a number of witnesses to his actions, as well as some of the boys involved, he still refused point-blank to acknowledge any such behaviour.

This is why confronting a paedophile who molested you as a child can be very frustrating and cause further pain. Instead of saying, 'I'm sorry;

what I did was wrong' etc., in the majority of cases the paedophile will completely deny the event(s) and may cause further hurt by getting other family members to believe them rather than you. One such case was that of a young man who went back to confront a Catholic priest who had molested him as a boy for several years. The priest still would not acknowledge what he had done and, in his confusion, anger and pain, the young man ended up committing suicide by burning himself. In a suicide note he stated that he felt that burning was the only way he could purify and transform both himself and his shattered past.

Paedophilia is the most common form of sexually deviant behaviour and results in the 20% of American children who are molested.[7] The common stereotype of the paedophile is that of a dirty old man or a Catholic priest, yet paedophiles are found in every religion, amongst all races, and in many different occupations, and especially wherever there are children. Yet they all have one thing in common: the desire for sexual gratification and sexual attraction to children.

Just as with the coach I mentioned above, paedophiles most often appear to be responsible, trustworthy, well-educated and upstanding members of the community, often with strong moral or religious beliefs. Yet this is a mask for a shadowy, manipulative character who feels more comfortable in the company of children whom he perceives as being less threatening than are adult relationships.

He may marry, and even have children or marry someone with children of their own, but usually this is simply a cover-up for his secret desires. Sexual dysfunction in the marriage is common. He typically prefers pre-pubescent boys or girls, or both. He will most often select children who appear lonely, troubled and in need of nurturing. He gradually feeds this need, often by providing time, toys, sweets, money etc. By doing this, he develops the child's trust and friendship, so that the child is often unaware how gradually gentle hugs and touches start taking on a more sexual overtone. Some paedophiles may be satisfied with simply watching a child undress, while others require more physical stimulation. Paedophiles will obviously be attracted to jobs that give them direct access to children – from playing Santa at the mall, to being a scoutmaster; they will create functions that necessitate interaction with children. They may also have many toys, games etc at their homes even if they don't have children.

Very often, a child will not reveal the nature of his or her relationship with a paedophile because the child may fear the repercussions from family, loss of the gifts, the relationship which is giving him/her attention and, in some cases ,because he/she may have been threatened into silence ('If you tell, I'll take away your pet/ hurt you or affect your family in some way.').

There appears to be no set formula which leads to someone's becoming a paedophile. Some have been abused as children and so repeat this learnt form of sexual behaviour – either as revenge for what was done to them and/or because children are an easy outlet for sexual expression where the paedophile feels unsure about himself in normal relationships. (It's easier to wield power and control over a child than an adult and this may be a way of re-enacting the paedophile's own childhood trauma.)

From this, a theory has arisen that paedophilia is genetic in origin; however, it seems more likely that the child who is abused will become an abuser, as an attempt to seek balance within the personality. Where he has mistrust, children trust; where he has denial, they have acceptance; where they are in their shadow selves, children aspire to light; where they have been victims, the child represents an easy way to be victorious; and where they are hidden and secretive, a child is open. Rather than seeking to heal their own wounded child, the paedophile takes the less courageous approach and wounds another.

Conduct disorders (such as excessive abuse, fighting, arson and stealing) as well as inappropriate intimacy, bed-wetting (from non-medical conditions) after the age of five, and cruelty to animals are all things which increase a child's likelihood of becoming a paedophile in later life. It must be stressed that not all children who have these problems become paedophiles; however, some or all of these traits occur in the childhood histories of most paedophiles.

Intimacy is about opening up our vulnerability to another person and sharing our inner self with them; in doing so we dissolve the self or the ego. If you say the word 'intimacy', it actually sounds like 'into me see'. A paedophile is afraid, and in most cases incapable, of true intimacy. He does not want someone to see inside to his true nature. Yet we all crave intimacy and the closest that the paedophile can get to this without being vulnerable is to be with children because, unlike adults, they do not threaten to see beyond his mask.

Rather like alcoholics, paedophiles can be treated but rarely are cured – either through conditioning treatments, male sex hormone reducers, associating negative situations with paedophiliac acts or therapies designed to deconstruct the erroneous thinking regarding their belief that the victim deserves to be treated in a certain manner. The urge to commit the act, however, will inevitably remain, although it is interesting that men who choose boys are approximately twice as likely to continue despite intervention, than are those who choose girls. (Morrison, 1995)

Female paedophiles usually only commit an offence if their partner is also a paedophile, though this is not always the case. In the majority of cases, they have been abused and molested in their childhood.

Sadomasochism

Theresa Berkeley was highly-skilled in the art of sadomasochism, keeping a large supply of fresh nettles and holly, straps of various shapes and lengths, whips, rods and many other tools of her trade at her house in Portland Place. But these paled in comparison to her great invention in 1828 – the Berkeley Horse or Chevalet. Essentially an adjustable ladder covered in padding, the client was tied to one side with his face and genitals protruding from the other. The 'governess' would then whip his buttocks, while an assistant in minimal clothing massaged his penis. The idea proved so popular that sales of the Chevalet earned Mrs Berkeley a small fortune.

The word 'sadomasochism' comes from the amalgamation of the names of the Marquis de Sade and Knight Leopold von Sacher-Masoch. It was Freud who linked the two concepts to form sadomasochism. Whilst sadism is sexual pleasure derived from cruelty and punishment inflicted on others, masochism is the opposite – a desire to have pain and force inflicted on one in order to achieve sexual gratification. A sadist without the balance of masochism can inflict much physical and psychological damage, whereas with sadomasochism, there are commonly certain rules which relate to the idea that you may be hurt, but you will not be permanently harmed.

Sadomasochism explores the depths of the connection between eroticism and power. *Femdom* is sadomasochism where women are the dominant partners. The male is often someone who holds a position of power in the world and yet who derives pleasure from having that power withdrawn. It is the paradox of power wanting to explore helplessness and deriving an erotic pleasure from doing so.

One in every ten people who read this book will have experimented in some way with sadomasochism. (So accepted is 'S&M,' that the American Psychiatric Association removed it from their Diagnostic and Statistical manual of Mental Disorders, in the 1980s.)[8] Its highest level of popularity is to be found amongst well-educated, middle- to upper-class people.

Being spanked or whipped, the use of blindfolds or restrictive outfits, humiliation in the form of forced defecation or urination are some of the methods used in sadomasochism, while masochists may abuse themselves by electrical shocks or self-mutilation. Choking oneself to achieve a more exhilarating orgasm is another method used by those who practice S&M.

Typically, sexually-masochistic behaviours will already be practised in some form in early adolescence and may have started in childhood in extreme forms of bullying, humiliation and deriving pleasure from causing others to suffer. This may well be a result of childhood abuse and trauma, where the victim now becomes the perpetrator in adulthood, as a way of avenging the past. He or she may have felt him/herself to be helpless to overcome sadistic behaviour and, in replicating this, seeks to overcome his or her own suppressed anxiety, anger and humiliation. By depersonalizing the victim, s/he attempts to depersonalize his or her own experiences.

For today's businessmen with A-type personalities (who have constantly had to put across a masculine, dominant, in control, successful, capable image), allowing themselves to explore the opposite role of feminine submission can be a way of reducing stress and experiencing an almost cathartic release. To feel free or out of control, one paradoxically needs to be bound and controlled. The experience of what one fears and tries to avoid (i.e. being disempowered) brings empowerment. It is a way of shedding the self that you have created and of finding peace through forsaking control. The pain is also a way of forgetting other concerns, such as deadlines, work-related problems and so on. For pain brings us into the moment. Just accidentally burn your hand and try to worry about your low sales figures at the same time!

S&M, then, can be said to be an imbalance of power which causes stress which can only be released though experiencing its opposite. For a child taught to feel shame about his/her body, being dominated can be a way of allowing his/her sexuality to be explored, without feeling that he/she is giving his/her consent as such. Having no control would allow him or her complete sexual expression instead of having to overcome feelings of guilt and shame in 'normal' sexual activities.

Voyeurism (scopophilia)

The voyeur gets sexually-aroused by witnessing others having sex or undressing etc. He or she may fantasize about doing these acts or may actually act upon them. Cinema, television, videos and (since the inception of the web) camcorders are a primary yet acceptable tool of voyeurism. We can watch as actors shower, undress, make love or masturbate – all from the safety of our lounge. So-called blue movies are a voyeuristic way of engaging in a sexual act in which we do not have to be intimate. You watch the experience and emotions yet are not part of them. Yet watching a blue movie or good film does not make you a voyeur in the traditional, paraphiliac, sense of the word. (Many years ago I recall a friend sending off for a blue movie advertised in the local newspaper, only to receive a video where the entire movie consisted of a blue screen!)

Sex, in its physical and emotional (as opposed to spiritual) form, as mentioned before, is very much to do with issues of power and control. In voyeurism, the voyeur is in a position of power and control, without risking any aspect of himself. He watches and feeds off the situation, yet gives nothing of himself to it. It's gratification without having to give anything away. It is a way of watching the vulnerability of others, yet not having to reveal your own, inner self. Perhaps in childhood one was forced to suppress one's sexuality and not able to express oneself emotionally. Watching others is a way of having the experience without the risk of losing control.

To some extent we are all voyeurs. Have you ever seen a roadside accident without people milling around or hanging out of their windows for a better view? Webcams that are placed in people's private spaces, often with unsuspecting participants, have played on this aspect and allowed others to profit from our fragile natures. Obviously, the desire is to empower ourselves to the point that we are not threatened by intimacy. At this level of inner growth, the desire to seek non-threatening views into the intimate world of others lessens; we want to experience it firsthand.

Endnotes

1 Hudson, Liam and Jacot, Bernadine, *The Way Men Think,* Yale University Press, Yale, 1992.

2 Do you know a Cross-dresser? www.tri-ess.org

3 Exhibitionism: *Psychology Today* cms.psychologytoday.com/conditions/exhibitionism.html

4 Fetishism: Catholic Encyclopedia www.newadvent.org/cathen/06052b.htm

5 As Freud described it in 1887, sexual fetishes in men are the result of childhood trauma regarding castration anxiety. www.jahsomic.com/SexualFetish.html

6 Paedophile: www.mental-health-matters.com and *Psychology Today* cms.psychologytoday.com/conditions/pedophilia.html

7 cms.psychologytoday.com/conditions/pedophilia.html

8 American Psychiatric Association: 1000 Wilson Boulevard, Suite 1825, Arlington, Va. 22209-3901. Phone: 703-907-7300 email: apa@psych.org *re* removing S&M from their Diagnostic and Statistical Manual of Mental Disorders in the 1980s.

Chapter Eight
Antics we get to do as we age

Habits of the elderly

They say that old age is not for sissies. Besides the physical deterioration of one's body, there are also the aches and pains that develop as well as the loss of strength and often short-term memory. How often do we use the expression 'burnt out?' As babies, we have an extraordinary amount of energy. Just watch a small baby and try to emulate its movements as it kicks, pulls, explores, attempts to roll over and so on. Children, too, have huge amounts of energy. They just can't seem to sit still, which is why it can be so exhausting as a parent trying to keep pace with your six-year-old. As we age, however, we seem to have less energy, and what ten years ago may have seemed a relatively simple task, now involves a far greater effort.

I love to windsurf but, as the years go by, the waves seem to get bigger each year, my wetsuit tighter and the wind stronger. In reality they haven't; it just seems that way. But the effort required to drive to the beach, rig up etc. just seems to get greater each year and, whereas at one stage nothing could keep me off the water, I now find I'm often grateful for an excuse to opt out.

But it's not only in sport that we notice our age; it's in memory loss, loss of confidence, we have less energy, get colder more easily, battle to adapt to the latest technology, need to have more 'power naps' and often lose our libido.

In this chapter, we examine some of the habits that creep into our routine as we age and we examine what the emotional symbolism of each habit might be. The overriding theme, however, is one of withdrawal. It's as if fully engaging in the world, so different from the one we were born into, has become too hard and so we gradually shut down the senses.

Forgetfulness

'Thanks for the memories…' the song goes, only, as one ages, one often can't remember the memories. You can recall the name of the first teddy bear you ever owned, but you completely forget your appointment with the dentist and you caused offence by mixing up the names of your children (and you only have two). It's called anterograde amnesia and it's when you can recall your childhood but have trouble remembering day to day events.

We know that people who experience traumatic events in childhood tend to obliterate them to the point that they will often have no recollection of them in later life. Sexual abuse falls into this category, as does war trauma etc. It is as if the mind is protecting one from re-experiencing the traumatic events and chooses rather to wipe out those events. When we lose our memories as we age, it is not that dissimilar. Subconsciously, we want to opt out rather than have to face the realities of life.

Often as we age, the future might not look that bright. We may know that a move into an old people's home is imminent; we may fear being alone, being financially dependent or losing our physical functioning. When life threatens us with all or some of these situations, not being there mentally may lessen the pain.

Take note of what it is you forget; this may give you a clue as to what issues are painful to you. When an art class I was giving suddenly became very full, I 'forgot' to send details to a couple of the participants, who then missed the classes. In my conscious mind I would never have done this – my subconscious mind, however, realized that a mental overload situation was approaching and so took charge.

How to improve memory

Emotionally, you may want to ask yourself if there is a pattern to what you forget. Could it be that you did not really want to do what you forgot? If it's someone's name that you always forget, ask what the nature of their relationship to you is. Not remembering someone can be an indication that you don't really want to interact with them. If it's certain events that you forget, the memory of them may be painful which is why shutting it out is preferable.

A typical diet does not always provide enough essential vitamins, particularly since, as we age, we tend not to eat as varied a diet simply because of the effort required to cook. This, combined with our body's ability to absorb fewer nutrients as we age, can result in deficiencies.

To function effectively, the brain requires a lot of energy. As we age, the neurons in the brain are less efficient in taking up glucose, the primary fuel of the brain. This energy decline causes memory and cognitive defects and eventually brain cells are destroyed. Memory loss is not something you simply have to accept. You can take action.

A number of supplements have been found to improve and restore memory function significantly and to slow down the ageing process. I suggest that you consult your medical practitioner for more information.

Hearing loss

Approximately one third of adults over the age of 65 suffer from hearing loss, varying from partial to complete. After the age of 75, the percentage increases to around 50%.[1] The reasons given are either *physical* disorders, which block the transmission of sound, or *functional* disorders, which result from psychological factors with no identifiable physical cause. Often, elderly people are reluctant to have a hearing test, either through fear or embarrassment and so may suffer silently for a number of years, unable to engage fully in conversation.

When our hearing is impaired, we are isolated from the rest of people. We battle to interact and our world becomes removed and remote. We *turn a deaf ear* to a world that we no longer want to *keep our ears open* to hear. Hearing is listening and we don't want to listen to others who tell us what we do not want to hear. I have heard it said by people who have hearing problems that the person they battle to hear most is their partner. This is very revealing, as perhaps this person is telling them things which they don't want to hear or do. Switching off from them then becomes a way of coping with the situation. It's a passive way of shutting out what we don't want to hear. Anger can also be involved, as in 'you cannot get me to hear what I don't want to.'

Parents yell at their children 'Listen to me!' when the child does not want to do what they have been told to do. Teenagers turn their music up so loud that they cut off every other sound in the house. 'Are you deaf?' we scream. Not hearing, then, is an act of defiance. We don't hear what we don't want to absorb and do. We want to cocoon ourselves in a world which no-one can invade; as we age, we find we cannot hear not only the things which we don't want to, but everything else as well.

It stands to reason that, as we age, we are less likely to want to listen to anyone else. To do so would be to submit to their will and not our own.

In not wanting to lose our sense of self, we regain our power by shutting them down. In the face of our deafness they are helpless to get us to obey them.

I once worked with a man who suffered from selective poor hearing. Each time he was asked to do something he did not want to do, he simply did not hear. However, at the slightest hint of something favourable he was *all ears!* I don't believe that this was a conscious action, merely a reaction to years of being made to listen and do what he did not want to.

There was a case I read of in the book *An Anthropologist on Mars*[2] where the author, Oliver Sacks, a surgeon, describes a patient cured of deafness after an operation, who, after hearing for a short while, shuts down his hearing emotionally and to all intents and purposes becomes deaf once more, even though there are no physical causes.

The incidence of children who have to have grommets or have ear problems appears to be on the increase. Perhaps the issues have to do with being forced to hear things that they don't want to hear, such as arguing parents, having to be obedient or being forced to listen to derogatory comments about themselves. Not listening then becomes a pattern of shutting out painful experiences, which as we age may result in deafness.

Another man's hearing ability decreased when his wife became interested in alternative healing. He found the whole concept absurd and the more she became involved in working in this field, the worse his hearing became. He couldn't grasp her new way of thinking and so chose subconsciously to shut it out.

I recall one elderly man who suffered from hearing problems saying 'why does everyone want to talk about uncomfortable issues, I can't understand it.' He had solved the problem for himself by having selective hearing. He filtered out all that could potentially upset him. When eventually he was pressurized into getting a hearing aid, he solved the problem by 'accidentally' standing on it and that was the end of that!

It may not just be others demands on us that we wish to shut out, but also their opinions. By *turning a deaf ear* we can avoid shutting off anything that we may find disagreeable. Our own negative thoughts may also block us from hearing the true nature of issues and the effect may worsen when we are emotionally stressed. Without hearing we can create our own peaceful world with no demands and little to upset us, hearing only what we choose to hear.

Ask yourself what it is that you may not want to hear, particularly if your ability to hear is worse with a particular person. Do they nag? Tell you what to do? Push emotional buttons? Why would you want to shut them out? Do you feel threatened or angry about what you have heard and want to shut it out?

Dippy with dementia

Dementia or senility is a breakdown of intellectual capacity which affects memory, judgement, confusion, and the ability to concentrate. It may bring on delusions and personality changes. It can be caused by a brain disease (such as Alzheimer's disease), a stroke, Parkinson's disease, Huntington's disease, Creutzfeldt-Jakob disease or AIDS-related dementia.

A long history of alcohol, smoking or drug abuse or exposure to poisonous gases can also cause dementia. Of people over the age of 70, about 10% can be expected to have serious memory-related problems, and about 50% of those (i.e. 5% in total) are due to Alzheimer's disease.[3] Alzheimer's disease is often slow to develop and may start out with difficulty in remembering recent events or in struggling to learn new things. It is often misdiagnosed and confused with severe depression, dehydration or over-medication.

You may forget things and not remember them again, whereas most people will recall forgotten things at a later stage. Things that were once easy to do may prove very hard; words may seem to slip away, causing both frustration and anger. Disorientation is common, as is misplacing things. Abrupt mood swings are also common and the sufferer may become more introverted. There may also be dramatic changes in one's personality, which may be very hard for loved ones to understand or cope with. Having some of these problems does not necessarily mean someone has Alzheimer's – they may be related to other, more treatable, problems. Consult your medical practitioner if in any doubt.

Strokes are the second major cause of dementia. Dementia or senility can be seen to be the symptom of an underlying problem. Although most of us regard senility as simply part of ageing, its physical causes may result from treatable factors. A medical investigation could reveal causes that a change in diet, lifestyle and additional supplements may slow down and, in some cases, even reverse.

As we age, we feel less physically and mentally powerful. We cannot walk the same distances, react at the same speed, indulge in vigorous all-night sex, have the same earning potential and generally do all the things we took so for granted in our youth. When we feel disempowered we feel insecure, hopeless and helpless. Our instinctive reaction is to attempt to control the world around us, as this makes us feel more secure. We feel too old to change ourselves in order to adapt to this new world, so attempting to control and change others becomes the preferred route – as in the grandmother who rules the family with a matriarchal rod of iron.

In tribal communities, the elders are revered as wise people with much to offer the tribe by way of passing on traditions and teachings. In modern society, however, old people are often simply considered a nuisance – past their 'sell by' date. With their children no longer living close by and pension funds often unable to keep pace with inflation, they are often left to eek out a lonely, impoverished and unloved existence, or are shoved into old people's homes, away from all that has been familiar to them. Their treasured pets, possessions and friends are often lost in the move, and even the strongest of people can become broken by the experience that no one really cares. Added to this may be the realization that this is it – all the goals that have not been achieved will remain unfulfilled – and that those things which they may have viewed as important in the past, such as a prestigious job, now in their waning days hold little real value. So many elderly people feel that they have wasted their lives, which only adds to feelings of vulnerability and worthlessness. The future may hold little hope in terms of love or finances, so it is not surprising that opting out of reality becomes a pleasant and preferred option. It is escapism from a world we no longer understand or want to inhabit.

We may also use the dementia as an opportunity to live out unfulfilled aspects of ourselves. The prim, spinsterish school teacher may indulge in provocative and sexually-lewd behaviour; the timid man may become violent and abusive. The pensioner who was never allowed free expression may suddenly become wild and do outrageous things, all in an attempt to balance the emotional imbalances experienced in his earlier life. Suddenly, we can do and say all the things we had to suppress before.

In feeling afraid and insecure, we revert to childish behaviour in an attempt to get the care, security and love we experienced as young children. By becoming once again children – being incontinent, irresponsible and incapable of caring for ourselves – we force society to do what it would otherwise not have done: look after us.

On the physical side, many of the suggestions given in the sections on deafness and forgetfulness may help. On the emotional side, others' demonstration of love and acceptance may go a long way to slowing down the process – i.e. if you are shown love and care you will not need to become childlike to demand it. Acceptance of one's limitations and focusing on the positive aspects of one's life will help in accepting the ageing process. Assisting others is a wonderful way of enhancing one's self-worth. Psychologist Elisabeth Kübler-Ross[4], who wrote books on death and dying and worked with the elderly and AIDS patients, started a wonderful program which brought the elderly together with orphaned babies. As the babies were held and loved they thrived, as did their aged caretakers.

Much of the sense of worthlessness that comes with age can be alleviated by being of service to others. It can be our gift back to the world before we pass on. My mother counselled into her seventies and, now in her eighties, delivers food to those in need. My father, who is ninety, sings in the choir and gives talks on the Bible's teachings. Other elderly people look after pets whose owners are away, get together to make clothes for the poor, read stories to children who've never have stories read to them, embark on their own and others' spiritual upliftment, nurture grandchildren whose parents are too busy to do so, or simply assist wherever they can. Each act of kindness to another is in truth an act of kindness to themselves, ensuring their self-worth and sanity.

Incontinence

For the last few years of her life, my grandmother rarely left our house without leaving a wet patch on the couch. Any hint as to her having done so and suggestions as to how to alleviate the problem were met with a steely denial. She simply would not admit that there was a problem. And, if there was no problem, no action needed to be taken.

She was quite a character and insisted on drinking only the strongest brewed beer, after which she was prone to stopping scantily clad women in the streets and telling them just what she thought of their provocative dress sense! Many a Sunday lunchtime, when she did not get her way with a certain issue, she would rise up from the table like a thundercloud and storm out of the door to make her way home. Woe betide my father, though, if he did not chase after her in the car and pacify her before bringing her back to crow triumphantly to my mother about her ability to manipulate her son, who should 'never have married. He should have stayed at home and looked after me.'! Over the years, she built up a strange mixture of friends and her renowned birthday parties included a range of well-known ballet dancers, the vicar (although she rarely went to church) and the motley crowd she had collected from the local pub.

There was the famous tale when, dressed in a green operating gown – open at the back with her sizeable backside exposed – she decided against having a hysterectomy and simply walked out of hospital and caught the bus home, green gown fluttering merrily in the breeze.

Returning, then, to the current behaviour of incontinence, it could be seen why my grand-mother had this problem, given years of living alone (her husband was killed in the First World War, when she was in her early twenties). She had been forced to bottle up so many emotions which, in the 'stiff upper lip' tradition of her environment, she could not share. Incontinence was a way of releasing all the unshed tears – a kind of letting-go, on a more subconscious level, of all her sadness.

Incontinence is a common problem with age, particularly in women, where muscles subjected to births and cutting are unable to contract as effectively as they did. Weakened with the strain of childbirth, these muscles symbolize an emotional weakening and feebleness, as years of unshed tears, loss, and concern for the future create pressure which is the forerunner of this collapse of efficient functioning. Water, in the body or elsewhere, symbolizes emotions. The moon, symbol of the feminine, controls the movements of the tides, and is seen as the dark, watery, intuitive side in contrast to the outgoing, fiery, masculine energy of the sun.

Consequently, being unable to hold on to our water or emotions can be symbolically seen as being unable to stem the tide of feelings that have built up over a lifetime. Where we held in our emotions, we no longer have the strength to do so; they simply pour out at will, increasing our feelings of lack of control and power in the world. Any confusion, grief or upset simply flows through us. The physical pressure we felt from a full bladder translates as the pressure we felt by carrying these emotions. As we age, the pressure becomes too much and we are forced to release.

As with all the previous behaviours, much can be achieved by adopting healthy forms of self-expression, building self-worth and working towards regaining the power we feel we have lost. The trouble is, this requires effort and strength of will, which can be hard to harness as we age.

Endnotes

1 Hearing loss: From Life Extension: www.lef.org/protocols/prtcl-055.shtml 'Nearly 16 million Americans are affected by hearing loss, ranging from temporary to permanent or from partial to complete (Bertoni et al. 2001). Hearing loss affects about 30% of all adults ages of 65-74. The percentage increases to 50% for adults by the time they reach age 75-79. Hearing loss is classified as conductive (external or middle ear disorders that block the transmission of sound); sensorineural (disorders of the inner ear or the eighth cranial nerve); mixed (a combination of conductive and sensorineural disorders); and functional (resulting from psychological factors and with no identifiable organic damage).'

2 Sacks, Oliver, *An Anthropologist on Mars,* Random House Audio, Unabridged edition, 1995.

3 Alzheimer's disease: Statistics on AD: AllRefer.com. Alzheimer's Disease.

4 From a live talk by Elisabeth Kübler-Ross in Cape Town.

Chapter Nine
Saying it like it is

Behaviour involving speech

A word on sound

In the beginning was the Word, and the Word was with God, and the Word was God.

John 1:1

When John wrote 'Word,' he was referring to the vibrating waves that cause sound or words to be. In the earliest translations from Aramaic, 'word' is closer in meaning to 'sound' or 'vibration' than an actual spoken word. When we speak, it is essentially a vibration of air past our vocal cords that creates the sounds that we hear. It is from the vibration of matter that the universe is created, in that everything is in a constant state of vibration. The smallest molecule is made up of vibrating or moving atoms, which create the illusion of something solid, much as a helicopter's blades look like a solid disc when rotating.

We and everything physical in the universe are constructed of atoms. When we speak, we create sound which, because everything else is vibrating, affects all aspects of the world around us. An opera singer's voice can reach a resonance capable of breaking a glass. Likewise, what and how we speak has a direct effect on all aspects of the world around us. Change the resonance of our voice or the way we speak and we change not only ourselves, but the world around us.

Sound can be said to have frequency (the number of complete cycles in one second) and amplitude (the depth or height of the pitch of the wave) as well as wavelength (the distance between any two adjacent corresponding points on the wave).

Sound is heard in terms of both volume and pitch. The volume depends on the amplitude of the wave. (The bigger the amplitude, the louder the sound.) The amplitude is also a measure of how much energy the wave has. The pitch of sound (how high the note is) depends on the

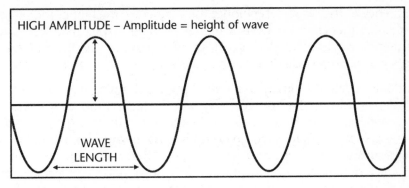

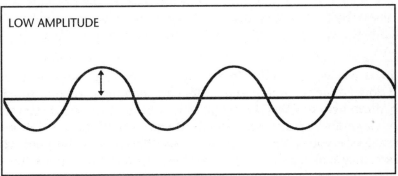

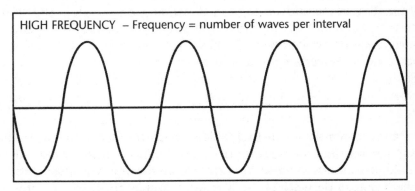

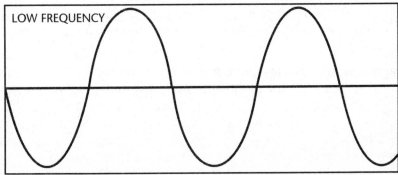

frequency of the wave. (The higher the frequency, the higher the pitch.) Higher frequencies also have a higher average power than do lower frequency waves. This doesn't mean that they are louder or have a higher peak amplitude: it just means that they have greater power.

To demonstrate this, imagine a line of people standing in a row of, say, 20 metres in front of a step. Starting with the first person, they stand up and then get down from this step, much as you do at a gym. As soon as the first person is finished going up and down the step, the next one starts, and so on down the row. The speed that they can move down the line is dependent on how quickly each individual person gets up and down, since the next person in line has to wait for the previous person to finish before he can move. This group movement, then, soon resembles a wave, much like the Mexican wave so popular at sporting events.

To make a wave with higher frequency, i.e. to make a wave that goes up and down more times in one minute, you need the people to stand up and down very quickly. This would obviously take more energy than if they were doing the exercise slowly. If you wanted the wave to move more slowly, you would tell them to take their time getting up, which means they would tire less quickly. Now, let's say that on one day the people are less energetic than on another day. Consequently, two different waves would be formed depending on the day, one using more energy and the other less. The amplitude, or the height of the wave, would be determined by how high the step is. A higher step would have greater amplitude but require more energy. The power of the wave is determined by how much energy the people have to expend to get up and down the step a number of times in one minute, etc.

It stands to reason, then, that if we replace the people in the above example with our voices, for our voices to carry greater amplitude it would take greater energy. What this means for us is that a person with a high amplitude would have a greater degree of energy, enterprise, courage and a stronger character than a person with a lower amplitude. A low amplitude person would have less energy and would lack get-up-and-go.

A high frequency relates to how psychically, artistically and musically attuned we are and how sensitive and attuned to the higher realms we are. The higher the frequency the voice has, the greater the potential to shift or change the vibrations of those around it. So, a high frequency sound has greater 'potential' and moves more quickly than its slower counterpart. In other words, the more spiritually-connected a person, the higher their frequency. This does not mean, though, that a person with a high frequency is necessarily very useful to society. They may have a low amplitude, in which case they could spend much of their time living lives of high moral standards, yet achieving very little. Likewise, someone with a high amplitude may be very powerful and thrive on developing new ideas etc. but, if they have a low frequency, they will not use their life to benefit those around them. An example of this would be Hitler, who had charisma and a high amplitude, but low vibration, – unlike, say, Christ who would have had both a high vibration and high amplitude. A low amplitude, low frequency person, will be neither strong in character nor high in spiritual morals.

Obviously, first prize is a high frequency and a high amplitude, if we are to have the dynamism and spiritual development to make the world a better place. Our wave-form is the actual shape of the wave that we have. This remains constant through lifetimes, while the amplitude and frequency may alter according to the lives we choose to lead.

Frequency, amplitude, wavelength and wave-form, when translated into our voice, reveal a great deal about us – whether our voice is high-pitched, gruff, soft or harsh. Different ethnic, language, religious and cultural backgrounds also determine a general way of speaking, revealing attributes of that particular group.

In Africa, certain tribal people speak very loudly, because of their heritage of life in open spaces where to converse with your next door neighbour requires a loud, resonant voice. In the UK, there is a wide variety of different ways of speaking, each of which reveals the area from which a person comes and the background in which they have been raised. We talk about having a *stiff upper lip,* so that we cannot mouth our speech or get all the sounds and feelings out. We can't *give someone lip* (it simply wouldn't be done!). Americans are known to be much louder than the British. Making a huge generalization, one could say that Americans en masse are far more abrasive and happier to say it like it is than are British people, who tend to hold back more. French is a much more flowing language and conveys the sensuality and sexuality of France. In comparison, German is a much more guttural and harsh-sounding language, mirroring the need for precision and a disciplined approach to life.

Two different wave-forms affect each other and create resonance. So my wave-form will affect yours and vice versa. Resonance creates harmony whereas discord creates disharmony. How you or I speak affects both of us and also indicates much about who we are. Consequently, it is not improbable but logical to infer that we can speak things into being, simply by creating the relevant wave-form. With this in mind, then, let's examine behaviour involving speech and sound and see what it reveals about our natures.

Garrulousness

Ever had a friend or colleague who could not stop talking? The weather, a pet, marital hassles, the best buys – the subject is immaterial; the chatter just never seems to stop. You may find them in boardrooms going on and on about a matter that has already reached resolution, or in book clubs where they seem to have read every book ever published, or in PTAs ensuring that the half-hour meeting takes at least double that time. In fact, garrulous people are to be found in every walk of life; some of us may even be married to one, particularly if we are the silent, introverted type.

After an encounter with a garrulous person, you come away feeling completely exhausted; the next time you see the person, chances are you'll dive into the nearest corridor or shop to avoid another onslaught. Yet garrulous people are not unpleasant people, rather they use speaking as a way to gain attention and control of a situation, because in many cases they are very needy people.

As we are all energetic beings, it stands to reason that energy flows from one person to another. If we feel depleted, we will seek someone to replenish us. If we cannot find someone and we cannot draw in energy from the universe, we will draw it from ourselves and, in time, doing so can make us ill. Being garrulous is a way of demanding attention, to replenish our resources, which is why it is so exhausting for the listener. The other day I came away from someone with whom I had an appointment that should have lasted twenty minutes at the longest. An hour later they were still talking and, in fact, were still doing so even as I walked out of the room to go to my next appointment. Whilst I felt drained, they clearly felt recharged. Now, by not sticking to my boundaries, I must add, I had allowed events to unfurl as they did and I take responsibility for that. What fascinated me, though, was that, had I not actually left, the person concerned would have carried on speaking for hours longer, oblivious to the one-sidedness of the conversation, so great was their need to be heard.

By not stopping talking we manipulate others to remain in our space, where we can energetically draw from them. If they threaten to leave, we introduce yet another topic or event to stop them, or else repeat what we have just said.

We all do this at some stage in our lives, but it takes a courageous person to admit that this is what is actually happening and to refrain from doing so and seek out other ways to regain lost energy. Relationships are constantly being rebalanced. If the seesaw drops too much to one side, then the other partner may well leave before they have been financially, emotionally, mentally or physically drained.

This is the sad aspect of garrulous people: their need drives others away and very often they cannot understand why people don't seem to like them. It's not essentially *them* that people don't like: just their energy-draining characteristic.

Talking abundantly is a way of releasing an excess of energy, usually caused by stress. Some clients will get onto my massage table and break into an unstoppable flow of thoughts and events. Doing this can also be a way of avoiding going into our feelings. By letting go of this energy, we attempt to release in a non-emotional way those emotions which we have suppressed. A lack of any real content in what they are saying is significant of garrulous people. There are all the details yet none of the actual emotions associated with the event they describe. By talking at length, we kid ourselves into believing that we have worked through an issue when, in truth ,by doing so we have neatly avoided having to deal with our feelings about it. Here we control not so much others, but our own emotions. Control, then, becomes more of a defence-mechanism.

We seek to communicate with others in order to avoid communicating deeply with ourselves.

The opposite of a garrulous person is the person who is too afraid to open up at all. Yet the wound may well be the same, and one person may display either of these opposing behaviours, depending on the particular situation.

If you are inclined to be garrulous, just remember that God gave us two ears and one mouth so that we could communicate in that ratio. Women typically tend to be more talkative than men and swing towards two-thirds speech and one-third listening; however, that is a generalization. Just remember, though, that if you do any more than your third of speaking, the chances are you could be starting to be a drain on those around you.

Interrupting

(See also Chapter Eleven, for interrupting in children)

Do you love to butt in, in the middle of someone else's sentence? Do you find yourself finishing your partners' story because you think you know it better or believe you tell it with more flair?

The word 'interrupt' comes from the Latin *inter* meaning 'between' and *ruptum,* from *rumpere,* which means 'to break' or 'to burst'. As with *rupt*ure, dis*rupt* and e*rupt* , the words indicate a less than harmonious break. Interrupting, then, is an indication that we are in some ways feeling hostile to those we choose to *go between.*

When a Billy-goat butts you, it is a clear message that he wants you out of his way. The interrupter is no different. He or she wants to butt in and sideline your impact on the conversation. Now, it's not simply that he or she wants centre stage: it's more an attempt to control what you have to say, often because they in some way resent not being able to control you completely. Cutting someone *short* is a way of be*little*ling them. Often, spouses will do this to their partner, through fear that their partner may say something of which they do not approve. This, too, is a method of control and indicates a lack of both respect and trust for the partner. The message is that, unless you say it my way, I'll ensure you don't say it at all.

Typically, the interrupter feels insecure and so seeks dominion over the world around him/her in order to feel in control. By not allowing you to voice your ideas or events, they ensure that they don't hear anything that would add to their anxiety. However, the practice does indicate a complete lack of respect for the boundaries of others.

Healthy boundaries come from having experienced health, stability, security and trust as a child. This gives us the ability to say, 'no, please stop that', 'I have eaten enough,' or 'this relationship is destructive and needs to end.' When our boundaries are not intact, we cannot respect the boundaries of others. We may swing from having rigid boundaries to lacking any at all, and are invariably dependent on others if we are to feel all right about who we are. Not being able to set our own limits, we will seek to merge with others to feel secure as we constantly seek to fill the emptiness we feel. We strive to make everyone else become the *enough* we seek.

By merging with other people's conversation, we devour them as a way to satiate our own need to be whole. This need may have arisen through poor bonding with our mother, trauma at birth, serious illness or surgery as a child, physical abuse, neglect, feeding difficulties or extreme poverty. It is a sad need for our wounds to be heard.

Speaking quickly

Like the garrulous speaker, the fast talker is seeking to get rid of excess energy. There is so much going on, and speaking quickly is a way of ridding oneself of it. Because of this, the communication can sometimes be scattered, as the speaker hops from one topic to another in an attempt to shed various issues.

Being a good communicator requires being an excellent listener. If I am so busy reeling off information to an audience, I cannot listen to, or be aware of, what it is they really want to hear.

Talking quickly can also be a sign of insecurity in that we want to get the talking over with as soon as possible. Perhaps we are unsure of our topic, or maybe we are very bright and need to process our thoughts as soon as they come to mind, irrespective of another's ability to comprehend what we are saying.

In order to overcome this behaviour, the speaker would need to spend more time listening to their inner, rather than outer, voice. This may quieten down this busy mind and bring it into greater balance.

Speaking loudly

When we feel small and insignificant, our ego attempts to mask this by appearing bigger than we feel ourselves to be. Talking loudly becomes a way of attempting not only to command attention, but also to rule or dominate by sound. Weaker voices are lost in the cacophony of noisy speech; we are attempting to make sure that this does not happen to ours. When people are drunk they often speak louder. Why? Because their egos are out in full force and demand attention. When sober, the ego would be suppressed. When egos are left to their own devices, they also crave control of the group. Speaking loudly affords them this luxury.

Speaking in a monotone

Speaking with very little amplitude or in a monotone is characteristic of someone who is afraid to extend themselves for fear of being either ridiculed or rejected. Instead of selecting from a vast array of expression, you suppress any emotion and what results is boring, lifeless speech.

Safe perhaps, but certainly nothing to set the world on fire. And setting the world on fire is precisely where the fear lies. 'Better to be safe than sorry,' you may say. 'Better to withhold my opinion than express it, in case it's wrong.' The result is a grey, but safe world. Boring not only the listener, but for you as well.

Enthusiasm in speech is the opposite of monotony. The word 'enthusiasm' comes from the Greek word *enthousiazein*, which meant 'to be possessed by a god'. When you withdraw enthusiasm from your speech, you indicate that you have withdrawn it from your life and have removed yourself from embracing divine or higher aspects of yourself. It's too scary to go there! Try injecting some enthusiasm into your speech and just see how your life changes!

Speaking through the nose

The nose is symbolic of personal recognition. When we speak through the nose, we speak through the desire to be recognized. Often this is because the nasal passages are blocked. This indicates that we have created blockages to being acknowledged or accepted. We want to receive recognition to enhance our self-worth, yet it does not come to us. When we have a cold, we speak through a blocked nose because we are sad (the mucus represents the inner tears) that we have not received unconditional love, approval and recognition for our efforts.

The need for recognition can be a very destructive force in our lives. Instead of doing what feels right for us, we act according to what we think others would want us to do. Doing so means that we are not being true to our own needs. The more we need the approval of others, the more it seems to elude us. When we learn to approve of ourselves, others do, too. This is the way it works, yet we try over and over again to get it to work the other way round. In this sense, we cause our own blocks to recognition.

Stuttering

Men and boys stutter more than their female counterparts – about four times as many men stutter than women. This may seem strange, as speaking is not gender specific – although, on the actual amount of words spoken, some may say that women win hands down. There is a body of evidence which says that stuttering is genetic and, indeed, around 60% of people who stutter have at least one other relative who does so, but this does not account for the remaining 40%. There is evidence to show that, in people who stutter, the left brain is not as dominant as it should be in language functioning and that there are also auditory problems or incorrect timing in the facial muscles.[3]

To some degree, we all have blocks in the fluency of our speech. We 'um' and 'arhh' our ways through many a conversation, without causing any concern. However, in the stutterer, these blocks in fluency become more obvious and may also involve facial tics, long silences, the stretching of sounds and inability to verbalize words completely.

History is littered with famous stutterers: Winston Churchill; the actor, Gerard Depardieu; Lewis Carroll; Marilyn Monroe; singer Carly Simon; King George, and a host of others. A clue to the emotional cause is that stutterers seldom stutter when they are acting on stage playing a role other than themselves. This curious information indicates that it is their own persona that they find hard to communicate or are unsure of.

Stutterers have been found to be much more sensitive than the general population, making them more intuitive and able to pick up on subtle emotions of others, which most people would not tune into. Being more sensitive also makes them feel more vulnerable and more under pressure to please others, because they would fear hurting or upsetting other people more.

There is also a sexual aspect to stuttering. In attempting to be what we feel others expect us to be in order to please them, much of our natural, instinctive behaviour is suppressed. Young adolescent boys are particularly prone to stuttering. As their hormones yo-yo and their sexuality comes to the fore, these sensitive young men can be unsure how to handle the changes, which cause them excruciating embarrassment. In attempting to suppress this wild, primal sexual, fiery emotional aspect of themselves and convey a more compliant and constricted view of themselves, these young men lose sense of who they really are. They are afraid to reveal what lurks in their shadow and consequently have difficulty in voicing or speaking up for themselves as the true self does not seem to be allowed to exist.

This outward 'nice' persona is confused with who we really are; stutterers in general may feel empty, inadequate and ill at ease with themselves. This can often come as the result of having a dominant parent who wants to mould us in a certain fashion. Wanting to please, we comply and then find it hard to distinguish between our needs and theirs. We greatly fear not fulfilling their needs as to who we should be. Put us on stage to be ourselves and there is little known self to be; we have no means to voice who we are and so fear and panic set in. But let a stutterer play a role and they are quite comfortable with being someone else. That persona is not them and therefore cannot be judged. There is no fear of not being good enough when one isn't oneself.

We may also have had a parent or parents who shamed us and continually criticized us for not meeting their needs. Feeling constantly deflated, one's own need would be to inflate oneself. This conflict then creates a tension – a bit like the dream of running away from the bogey man and being frozen to the spot – where our words become frozen. The result is a huge amount of frustration and insecurity.

Assisting stutterers more commonly involves management of the problem, rather than a complete cure. Reducing tension and learning fluency-enhancing skills has been shown to help. Working at ways to enhance self-image and understanding and becoming confident in who you are also go a long way towards minimizing stuttering. Basically, what helps is learning to be and play the role of yourself and be okay with who you are by building self-esteem.

If you do know someone who stutters, you can assist them by making a concerted effort to relax both yourself and them in your company. Never give advice such as 'slow down', etc. and don't interrupt or finish the sentence or word for them. This only serves to disempower the stutterer. Maintain eye-contact and really listen to what the person is saying, as opposed to becoming bored and looking at the great blonde just passing by! Stutterers are of normal, and often above-average, intelligence; don't treat them as morons or in a patronizing manner.

Whining

Whining was originally associated only with dogs and meant 'to complain in a feeble way'. Dogs being our inferiors, according to their pack mentality, are less empowered than ourselves. We decide when they can go for a walk, what and when they can eat and even if and when they can mate. We pretty much rule their lives completely. When a person whines, it is an indication that, like their doggy pals, they feel completely disempowered to take any constructive action to achieve what they want and must rely on making us feel guilty, if they are to succeed in their desire.

It's a cry for help or love. People who whine feel incapable of helping themselves and must rely on those whom they see as being stronger to assist them. Unable to voice their needs clearly, they are reduced to using manipulation and emotional blackmail to achieve their end. They are victims who feel powerless to assume responsibility for their own lives and, like a small child, are looking for a maternal or paternal figure to protect and provide for them. To do this they need you to feel sorry for them, much as the pictures of large-eyed puppies and kittens on posters implore you to take them home.

To overcome the victim-mentality, one needs to assume responsibility for one's own life as opposed to blaming others for it. So often we avoid giving our children responsibilities (such as feeding the dog or doing the washing up) yet it is these responsibilities that build self-esteem, which is essential if we are to grow beyond a victim-mentality.

Endnotes

[1] The Stuttering Foundation '... (approximately 60% of those who stutter have a family member who does also)... Stuttering affects four times as many males as females.' The Stuttering Foundation of America maintains a toll-free hotline on Stuttering (800)992-9392 or (901)452-7343. Call for free information brochures and a nationwide referral list of speech-language pathologists who specialize in stuttering. info@stutteringhelp.org. Stuttering Foundation of America, 3100 Walnut Grove Road, Suite 603, P.O. Box 11749 Memphis, TN 38111-0749.

Chapter Ten
Horrendous habits

Bizarre and unusual habits

'Every time I go to a restaurant, I have the habit of grinding the pepper grinder really well under the table, before I'll put any pepper on my food. I am very concerned that the grinder may be dirty. Why does this worry me so?'

I was being interviewed about habits for a radio talk-show. I felt confident that I could field the majority of queries about common habits, such as nail-biting and teeth grinding, off the cuff. The talk-show host waited expectantly, as did the thousands of listeners, for words of deep profundity to pour forth. In those few, painful seconds, I twirled my hair until it resembled ringlets! Eventually, a few sparks of wisdom were ignited and I was able to give a reasonable, if not brilliant, response.

Since then, however, I have become aware of many unusual habits – most of them that few would admit to and some that one would find hard to conceive! Although not common to many people, there may be some resemblance to a habit that you or someone close to you has, so delving into the strange and bizarre may prove insightful!

The toe-twiddling interviewer

The newsreader was just finishing his radio broadcast as the interviewer and I, perched on high chairs, microphones beaming towards us, sat ready for the start of the show. I watched, fascinated, as the interviewer started to twiddle her toes. She was perched on the stool, sandals on the floor and with one foot tucked under her rear; she had easy access to her toes. Noticing the direction of my gaze, she asked me in hushed tones why she always did that before going on air. My answer was that toes represent our ideas, thoughts and concepts. Prior to going on the phone-in show, she clearly had to draw in or stimulate as much brain activity as she could in order to control the show successfully.

Playing with her toes was literally like giving her thinking a quick workout. A reflexologist knows that the whole body is mirrored in the feet, with the toes being like small heads, each of which represent a different aspect of our thoughts. The big toe relates to thoughts about spirituality, our analytical aspect and intellect, as well as our intuition. Had she been playing only with her second toe, the interviewer's thoughts may have had to do with love or the amount of self-love she had, or with a persona which she wanted to project over the air. Twiddling the third toe would have been stimulating her ability to react and her self-esteem; the third toe relates to communication and her ability to react to questions and calls. The fourth toe concerns ideas and beliefs to do with relationships, money, sex and the ability to communicate ideas, while the small toe would relate more to the interviewer's thoughts about the listening audience in general.

Understanding this, then, it became easy to see why playing with her toes had become such a habit prior to going on air. Fortunately for her, she was not a TV interviewer – which may have caused a few raised eyebrows had she indulged in her habit!

The man who pulled his trousers...

Daniela asked: 'Every time my husband and I have an argument, he keeps yanking at the front of his trousers. Why?'

Ever heard the expression 'I wear the pants around here'? As her husband became increasingly frustrated at Daniela's determination not to adopt his point of view during a fight, he was forced to act out what he really wanted to say, which was: 'Hey! I'm in charge. Look, I'm the one wearing the pants. Look. Look!' When she persisted in not submitting, his tugs became more frantic, as his subconscious acted out a program that had most likely been written into him as a child. 'Men must wear the pants. Look, I'm wearing them here!'

...and the man who played with his crotch

'Every time my boss would come to speak to me or one of the other female colleagues, his hand would move to his crotch and he would move it around there,' said Anna, an attractive sales employee. 'I don't think he was aware of what he was doing; it would be too embarrassing knowing that you were doing that. I feel it was just a nervous reaction. I hope he wasn't duping me all that time!'

Anna's employer was not much different from the husband who played with his trousers. He was affirming both to the women he worked with and to himself, 'Look, I have the penis. That means I rule here. Listen to me. I have the power.' (Which, of course, showed that he was concerned whether he actually did.)

Squeezing other people's blackheads and pimples

One caller mentioned how she enjoyed squishing her son and husband's pimples. I asked around and found that the practice is not as uncommon as one might believe. It became clear that the satisfaction of squishing the white gunk out proved to be close to exhilarating. Gross, you might feel, but not if we look at other animals. My cats lick each other lovingly; apes spend hours combing each other for fleas and other parasites. It's sort of a natural, albeit primal, way to behave.

Pimples represent our anger and conflict that builds to a head and erupts. That is why they so often happen when we are teenagers. We can experience much inner torment at this time, which can develop into a dislike of self. Emotions and hormones surge unstoppably through our bodies, causing mood-swings and embarrassing sexual urges that can't be fulfilled. These erupt as small expressions of our inner torment. The face is where we face the world. If covered with acne, we face the world full of self-loathing and shame for the emotions and urges that we can't contain. The blackheads are the hardened, blackened dirt or 'stuff' that has become stuck and blocks the free flow of the breathing of the skin.

As well as fulfilling a primal urge of grooming and caring, as a mother or lover, squeezing someone's pimples is an attempt to assist them to release what is defacing them – to try to make things right. In squeezing out the poisons, the skin and person can heal. Skin is a means of connecting to the outside world. When we see what we don't like (such as a pimple) on one we love, our reaction (if we are nurturing) is to want to remove the blemish and the small outpouring of anger that it represents.

Shaving or cutting our pubic hair

French waxing is probably one of the more popular of bizarre habits; it is considered to be a huge turn-on for many men. To see a vagina in its shaven, exposed vulnerability allows men to feel that they are conquering a young virgin and adds a new dimension to what may have become a rather boring sex life.

However, there are women who cut their pubic hair more out of compulsion than for sexual reasons. It just feels good to have less hair. Our hair is vital as a receptor and cleansing mechanism for the body. We sweat more when we have hair and, consequently, get rid of more toxins. Yet women seem to have a compulsion for shaving off all their bodily hair – from their legs to their armpits, to tweezing their eyebrows and waxing their pubic hair. Bodily hair is seen as a masculine attribute; therefore, by ridding ourselves of it, we believe ourselves to be more feminine.

Yet true, primal femininity is by its nature hidden, warm, mushy and moist with strong yet seductive odours. In ridding ourselves of our bodily hair, we seek to rid ourselves of our primal nature. Everything must be smooth and smell of synthetic deodorant for fear that our musky sexual nature might be smelt. Cutting off our pubic hair becomes a way of retreating into the virgin child state, where all is clean and pure with not a hint of our sexuality visible.

Hair also acts as an antenna for the body. We draw in energy from it and release unwanted toxins via it. In the Bible, Samson needed his long hair in order to maintain his strength or symbolic spiritual connection. Our hair stretches from the physical body into the astral or emotional body. Here we can access other emotional dimensions. Cutting our pubic hair, then, cuts us off from our emotional/sexual body.

Through abuse or shame we may be afraid to want to be sexual. The hairiness of our body reminds us of our sexual nature, as opposed to the innocent hairlessness of a child. Rather than acknowledge this, we seek to remove all trace of our adult desires.

Bumping into people

I had asked my daughter to do some chores for me when I became aware that she was bumping into me. I also recall an employee who used to shove into me when I was cooking in the kitchen, supposedly 'accidentally'. When I was asked by someone else what this meant, I could recall the incidents and so relate to the behaviour which she described.

Bumping into someone, in this context, is an act of aggression. Small boys shove each other in queues as a means of defining their order in the pack. The same is true of adults. We want to tell someone to *push-off*. To mark-out our territory by shoving them to one side lets them know that we are both irritated by them and not intimidated. In doing so, we *push our luck* and hope that they won't retaliate. Just as a pusher forces drugs upon us, we push others, hoping to intimidate them into submission.

Sex and the bizarre

Sex is undoubtedly the area where bizarre behaviour is most prevalent. From old ladies watching naked young men ride training bicycles, to the report of a man who, once stripped to his socks, paid a prostitute to allow him to throw cream buns at her – there seems no limit to what people find arousing.

Through the ages, contraception methods have sometimes been extremely bizarre, from mouse-dung applied in the form of a lotion, to a tasty potion of snail-droppings, wine and oil or the wearing of a weasel's testicles on one's thighs. After that lot, it's understandable that no-one would find you at all desirable!

Sneezing after sex to expel the semen, or inserting pepper into the mouth of the uterus were also popular forms of contraception during Roman times.

Unusual sexual behaviour is covered in greater detail in Chapter Seven.

The man who banged his head

(See also Chapter Eleven, for head-banging in children.)

Chris was a bright, ambitious young man who had plans to make it big in the advertising world. However, he lacked much of the ability required to excel in this highly-competitive arena. This caused his ego and inadequacy to clash frequently, making him on the one hand charming and, on the other, moody and belligerent.

To make matters worse, his manager was a woman, which did little to appease his frustrated ego. He developed a strange habit of banging his head against the office partitioning every time he was asked to perform a task that he did not want to do. In retail advertising, changes are par for the course and Chris did not like changes. Consequently, he spent a huge amount of time banging his head. He literally felt himself to be banging his head against a wall – fortunately for him it was not made of bricks! *(See also self-harming, in Chapter Fourteen.)*

Babies often bang their heads as a way of comforting themselves. It's as if the knocking movement mirrors the rocking of their mother. Usually, they outgrow this behaviour; however, the link between banging and comfort may not always be broken. So, while Chris's banging may have served to convey his frustration to his manager and colleagues (which he was unable to do verbally), it could also have brought with it the comforting security of a subconscious message that said: 'hush now; all this will be all right.'

Hoarding

An old English saying goes, 'there's none so queer as folk.' Hoarders must surely fall into this category given the bizarre items that people choose to hoard. Now, it's perfectly acceptable to hang on to your size 8s from ten years ago, hoping that by some miracle you'll shrink from your size 14s to fit them again, but it is another matter to collect every newspaper or magazine you've ever read. Most of us have some hoarding potential. However, when taken to extremes, it falls into the category of an Obsessive Compulsive Disorder, rather than simply a reluctance to throw away something which may be useful in the future. (Why is that, no sooner than we have thrown something away, we need it?)

My grandfather, who was in every other way perfectly able to throw away what he didn't need, had a thing about old cheque-book stubs. He died at 94, leaving behind numerous boxes containing every cheque stub from the last 70 years! Known as pack-rats, and often viewed as eccentrics, hoarders may find themselves knee-deep in possessions or just plain trash that they have been unable to throw away. In extreme forms, this can become very incapacitating and result in isolation as a consequence of the clutter that the hoarder is embarrassed about, yet unable to clear. The television programme, *How Clean is Your House,* demonstrates this. Interestingly enough, even when they do require a particular item, hoarders are seldom able to find it amongst the mess, making the purpose of hoarding rather futile. In extreme cases, homes can look as if they have been vandalized, as waste debris is strewn over every available surface.

One of the most famous cases of hoarding was that of Langley Collyer, an admiralty lawyer, who lived with his brother, Homer, an engineer, in a luxurious three-storey mansion at Fifth Avenue and 128th Street, Manhattan. Between 1933 and 1948, they managed to fill the mansion with 103 tons of junk and refuse, which included 11 pianos, a primitive X-ray machine and the components of an entire Model T Ford. At night, Langley would walk the streets searching for items to hoard. He died pathetically when a pile of items he had constructed to fall on any intruder crushed, not a robber, but himself.[1]

Hoarding is all about fear, control, holding on to the past or the belief that, if an item is thrown away, something bad may occur. Whilst we hold on to things, we feel that our world will not change and that makes us feel safer. Afraid to let go of the past, we hang on to items that represent it. Letting those go amounts to letting go parts of ourselves – a thing which we are understandably afraid to do.

The amount hoarded can accumulate to the point where the house or flat becomes a health and fire hazard.

Typical hoarding symptoms that are usually linked to Obsessive Compulsive Disorder include:

- Purchasing large amounts of items to store for future use – a kind of doomsday need

- Not throwing away useless or broken items

- Not possibly being able to use the quantity of items of a particular type one has purchased – such as hundreds of bars of soap

- Keeping old newspapers and magazines, which may never have been read

- Not throwing anything away for fear that you may need it one day

- Going to the dustbin and retrieving items which others have discarded

It is inherent in many of us to hoard, particularly if we had parents who may have suffered a lack, either as a result of a war or poverty. This message of 'waste not, want not' can get taken to extremes. Many animals hoard food in summer to last through winter months and the principal remains the same in us humans. We fear that, when times are not as good, we may need what we have thrown away, so we hold on to things rather than trust in the future to provide abundance.

Some of us hoard **sentimental** items – such as old school reports, baby blankets or just about anything that you can relate to an event, place or person. This type of hoarding may be compounded if the person fears growing up and wants to hold on to the past, be it childhood or a relationship. It is not uncommon after a death to keep not only the room of the deceased, but all its possessions, intact for years. Letting go is just too hard to do. There may also be a superstition that getting rid of these old things will offend the person who has died and in some way cause bad luck. In letting go, the hoarder fears that a part of themselves will be lost.

Then there is the person who is **hyper-responsible,** or the hyper-caring hoarder, who believes that whatever they don't throw away could be useful to another, so they hang on to all these items, waiting for the right needy person to appear. They would feel guilt for throwing away a potentially useful item. In reality, most of the things prove to be broken beyond repair or badly damaged and not worth fixing. (I acknowledge this when I think of the yogurt maker without instructions, electric knife sharpener and fizzy-drink maker which leaks gas and thus does not fizz, that I have acquired!)

Hoarders invariably find it very hard to make **decisions** as to what should be kept and what should be thrown away. Rather than make the decision, they hold on to the item and avoid doing so. That way, they ensure that they won't fail by throwing something useful away. The fear here lies more in the fear of failing to make the right choice.

Organization is also a frequently-cited problem. The hoarder just can't fathom out a logical way to file or store objects, so he maintains disorder – such as piles of objects all over the place in which, paradoxically, he feels some sense of order. By placing all objects within view, he or she believes that they will be able to find what they need when they need it.

Then there may be the hoarders who believe that, in throwing a magazine away, some vital article may also get lost. Likewise, an envelope thrown away may contain money or some other vital item. Rather than check everything, which is hugely time-consuming, it becomes easier just to keep it. When you throw an object away, you no longer have control over what happens to it; consequently, hoarding can be seen to be a desire to **control**.

This control may take the form of a fear of forgetting. If we forget an item we have read, keeping it somewhere gives us the opportunity to re-read it. We can't possibly remember everything we have read, yet in the desire to do so, the hoarder feels obliged not to part with any information. Once discarded, they fear that they may forget the content or the object's appearance and it may be gone forever.

Other hoarders 'specialize' in making collections of items in order to achieve a deep sense of satisfaction when the collection is complete. However, this rarely occurs and the reward is seldom realized. Others collect mental information or make notes about issues which will seldom if ever be reread.

Assisting hoarders to let go may be difficult and require much patience and understanding. They need to be gradually encouraged to part with items. Perhaps rules and boundaries also need to be established – such as, if you haven't used it for at least a year then get rid of it. Methods for organizing and then maintaining that organization need to be established if the results are to be long-term. Rather than experiencing fear from having released their 'stuff', many hoarders feel a huge relief for having done so. Take the lady who was persuaded to throw away all her old and dated sewing patterns: 'I literally felt like I had lost my old patterns in an emotional and physical sense. I felt I could start afresh. It was an amazing experience!'

The process of releasing involves four definite actions:

1. Throwing it away

2. Recycling

3. Giving it away

4. Putting it away.

No other, in-between, actions should be entered into. For example, if you have a 12-year-old book on fondue cooking, ask yourself if you have a fondue pot. No? Well then, do you know a friend who has? No? Option 2 makes no sense, nor do 3 and 4, therefore option 1 is the solution. So throw it away.

Hoarding – Animals

In April 1993, Vicki Kittles was found living on a filthy bus in Astoria, Oregon, with 115 dogs, four cats and two chickens. The animals were all dying slow and horrible deaths from starvation and disease. Ms Kittles swore that she loved the animals and that they were well cared-for; the reality proved otherwise. It was not the first time that Ms Kittles had run foul of the law; she had previously been found in Florida living in a house full of animals (including two horses kept in a bedroom), animal faeces and carcasses of animals that had starved to death. Although extreme, Ms Kittles' example of animal hoarding is not uncommon.[2]

It is a sad and awful occurrence from people who believe they truly love animals. I came across a similar situation in Zimbabwe years ago, where an old lady kept hoards of cats. Although on a farm and having more space, the cats had inbred to the point where most of them were deformed and many blind.

Typical animal hoarders fail to recognize, or refuse to acknowledge, that the animals they are supposedly caring for are grossly neglected. They will stubbornly refuse to part with any of their animals, no matter how ill or starved they may be, and deny the reality of the situation. They will argue at length that animals kept in small cages do not suffer or that overcrowding is not a problem for animals. There may be a marked contrast between how they portray themselves in the outside world and how they live privately. They are very hard to cure and will inevitably return to their habits as soon as they can.

So what motivates this habit? A clue lies in the sympathy they like attracting for the 'good work' that they are doing. This feeds their need to appear good when their dark shadow-side threatens to emerge. They develop a hero/martyr archetype with publicity that makes them feel more important and noble than their fellow man. Becoming enamoured of the persona they have created, they are loathe to cloud it, e.g. by using euthanasia on any of the animals.

Control is also a major issue. In their own lives they may have experienced or felt little control or power; now they rule the roost and have power over the poor unfortunate animals in their custody.

Some have a warped view that any life is better than no life. So, rather than put down the suffering animal, they extend its life albeit miserably. Often, they then boast about how they have 'saved' the animal and deny condemning it to a fate worse than death. They are often intelligent and scheming people; they can manipulate the media and benefactors extremely well.

An animal hoarder is often a single, lonely lady who collects cats or dogs until the situation gets out of hand. This becomes an obsession, and reality starts to become blurred so that she may not be conscious that the living conditions have become unspeakably filthy. For the animals that she intended to help and rescue, in some cases life becomes one of terrible suffering, often leading to death by illness, inbreeding or starvation.

Most often animal hoarders are middle-aged to elderly, white, female and (ironically) may work in caring or teaching professions. They may appear perfectly normal in their professional lives, or only mildly eccentric. They have often had chaotic childhoods with unstable parents and look to animals for the love which they crave. It is reported that there may be thousands, if not tens of thousands, of hoarders in the USA alone.

Picking your nose

This is a very common habit which, like bum-scratching, is not one we are inclined to admit to. Now, most of us have had a good dig at times but, for some people, the behaviour has become ingrained and any spare moment whilst driving (for instance) will find them digging deep into the recesses of their nose.

The nose is associated with recognition. It is what we see most prominently on the face of another person. It sticks out and shows just where we push ourselves into the world, as in being *nosey* when it comes to becoming involved in the business of others. We use it to breathe or take in the world and it can become blocked when we do not want to interact with others, such as when we have a cold and want to shut ourselves off from the world for a while. However, sometimes we feel that there may be a blockage in how we are being received by others or recognized for our efforts. Then we seek to remove this blockage by picking our nose and clearing the air passage in order to receive better from others.

Worse still are those who eat their pickings. Now, why would you want to take all the dirt that your mucus has stopped from being taken into your system and ingest it? Perhaps because you want to eat up that which has been blocking or hindering your acceptance. By eating it, you are assured that it cannot *get up your nose* again.

Endnotes

[1] Useless information: http://earthdude1.tripod.com/collyer/collyer.html The case of the Collyer brothers

[2] Animal hoarders: www.vetcentric.com/magazine/magazineArticle.cfm by Wes Alwan: story of Vicki Kittles

Chapter Eleven
Tots and tantrums

Children's behaviour

As uncomfortable as it might be for us adults, dogs and children often express, through habits, the emotionally-suppressed issues of their owners or parents. 'Oh, my goodness,' you may respond, as images of your five-year-old's perverse habit of eating snot or your hound's loving indulgence in compulsively licking his balls, come to mind! The truth is that, in a family environment, we are not separate islands floating in a vast sea of indifference. As author Denise Lynn so aptly put it, we are all 'tied together by our cosmic shoelaces.'

In a family, some people may choose to express disturbing issues while others repress them. Children and pets are less skilled at repressing their feelings, so they are more likely to show that something is amiss through their behaviour. Or haven't you ever had your normally exemplarily-behaved children turn into monsters just as your in-laws arrived? Often, the more sensitive child is the antenna for the family's tension and expresses this by acting out.

Imagine a U-pipe filled with water and with a plastic bottle at either end. If you squeeze the one bottle, the water will appear in the other and vice versa. It's no different in families. In school, we learnt that matter can't be lost; it can merely be changed from one form to another. The same holds true for emotions. They do not disappear but the tension can shift. When an unhelpful houseguest arrived to stay, after a few days, my dog suddenly started attacking other dogs, only to become placid after the much waited-for departure. There was no mystery here as to where my unexpressed anger was being channelled!

We can also have this stress imbedded in our psyche, as I found out some years ago, when I went to a psychic/hypnotherapist. He took me back into past traumatic experiences that held repressed emotions. One incident involved a scene in my grandmother's house, when I was a small baby. My mother was holding me in her arms while she cried. Later, I asked my mother if she recalled any such incident, as I was too small to remember either the incident or the cause of her grief. She replied that she did and could tell me what had upset her so much. This was a clear indication to me that her anguish had in some way influenced my emotional make-up, and the hypnotherapist had been able to pick up the effects.

This chapter, though, is not about beating ourselves up as adults for our inadequate parenting skills (most parents try their best); rather, it's about understanding that your child's individual habit may *also* involve the family as a whole. Through understanding this, you may be able to assist not only your *child* to heal emotionally, but also your *family.* No living person is without his or her issues. Life is not easy but, by accepting our imperfection rather than burying it in denial, we can begin to heal not only our own wounds, but also those of the people with whom we live.

Bed-wetting

'No sooner does my four-year-old son crawl into our bed, than we find ourselves experiencing a warm and very wet sensation. He seldom wets his own bed, and this has happened enough times to make me realize that it's become a habit. Why does he do this?'

The mother looked exhausted and close to tears. Now, one could argue that having got up from sleep, her son's bladder was full and the change in environment brought about this sudden and unwelcome response. This may have been a physical contributory factor, but the fact that he seldom wet his own bed suggested that, emotionally, something else was at play.

For centuries, sailors have regarded the sea as a maternal presence, one moment calm and alluring and the next wild and tempestuous. The sea relates to the feminine and female issues – such as feeling, as opposed to thinking. We cannot see what is hidden at the bottom of the ocean, so water represents both our emotions and the unconscious. When we cry, we release these emotions in the form of tears, just as a build-up in electrical static in the air causes thunderstorms and rain. It is extremely healing to cry. However, we are brought up in a society where many little boys still have drummed into them the words: 'Boys don't cry.' Even if not consciously verbalized, the message remains an unspoken rule in many households, if boys are to win their father's approval. So what happens to these repressed feelings in a child? They build up and the subconscious finds an alternative way of expressing them, through bed-wetting.

Just as the tears which they represent, bouts of bed-wetting indicate that there is something in the child's life that is upsetting him/her deeply. In the case mentioned above, by releasing this angst or emotional backlog in his parent's bed, the boy was unconsciously seeking to draw their attention to his fears. It was a cry for help that his understandably irate parents were unable to hear, and so the pattern repeated itself.

The fact that bed-wetting occurs at night is an indication that the child may not be conscious of his/her fear, which makes it all the more confusing for the child. Asking a child what is the matter may not bring about any indicative response, as the fears may be subconscious.

Fear is often disguised as anger, like animals who attack when trapped. A cornered dog will attack another dog or person who comes near it. Likewise, a child can be afraid and angry at the same time. The phrase *pissed off* combines both anger and release in one expression. The child may be extremely angry at whoever has caused them so much angst. Bed-wetting is a way to release both the fear and the anger. Ask yourself why or with whom your child may be angry.

If your child is bed-wetting, examine their playgroup/school environment. Could they be afraid of someone? Are they being bullied? Has there recently been a divorce or major upheaval that may have threatened their security? Is it possible that the child may be suffering some form of abuse? There may be deep guilt or shame involved that the child has no other means of expressing. Is the child being victimized at school, or at home by siblings? Could the child be afraid of one of its parents? Commonly, this is the father. If the parent is very strict and authoritarian, the child may be very scared of causing displeasure, which causes fear and tension. The emotional pressure that the child experiences during the day builds up and, if the child has no other means of releasing it, bed-wetting provides a solution. It also allows the child to turn the tables on his or her empowered parents and disempower them. However, we must not forget that, like tears, bed-wetting is a cry from the subconscious for help.

When we are afraid, both animals and humans may urinate spontaneously. As the urine is released, so is some of their fear. Bed-wetting is similar. Consequently, if it occurs regularly, it should be treated with compassionate concern and opportunities created for the child to express their feelings, perhaps with the help of a therapist. Sensitivity to the child's needs must be of prime concern. It must be emphasized that discipline is the worst possible reaction and will only add to the shame and fear.

Bragging

When we feel deflated, we seek opportunities to inflate ourselves. While a degree of bragging is common in many children, when it reaches alarming proportions, it is an indicator that the child's self-esteem is at a low ebb. Often, this is a phase and not a cause for great concern. However, it should be monitored, as a bragging child is tolerable, but an adult who can't stop adding noughts and inches to everything he or she speaks about, is a good reason to leave the vicinity quickly.

Carting children to and from school and on school outings, I am aware of the children who are so desperate for some degree of self-esteem that they seldom miss an opportunity to boost their little egos. Because it is an ego-related issue, much of their desire to inflate themselves is won at the expense of the person with whom they are interacting, which is why they are seldom popular. If we are too full of ourselves, we cannot relate deeply to another person – there is no space! As the line between bragging and lying is very thin, another reason why kids who brag are not liked is that no one can really trust them.

Relationships, even at a young age, are founded on trust, which is why it is hard to have a meaningful relationship with someone who tells whoppers. If a child is allowed to brag unrestrainedly over a long period, it's easy to see that they could come to start believing their own exaggerated distortions of the truth. If others are impressed, a pattern is put in place which basically says, 'I am not good enough as I am; therefore I need to continuously add and exaggerate in order to be okay.' A child, and later adult, can then seldom ever be happy, as they never feel worthy simply just being who they are. They also live in fear that someone is going to find out and burst their inflated bubble of untruths.

Because the self-esteem is low, the ego gets to run rampant, which over time can result in other behavioural problems, such as an explosive temper. The ego's needs have to be fulfilled and the craving becomes the driving force in the individual's life. We can never then simply be human beings: we feel we have to be humans doings.

If your child brags, look for ways to gently and genuinely boost his or her self-esteem, without exaggerating their achievements. If your child is lousy at sport, perhaps the child has another talent which allows him or her to feel accepted and successful. As a parent, are you over critical? Are your expectations of your child too high?

Bullying

I'm not sure which is worse: being told that your child is a bully, or having your child be the victim of bullying. Originally, the word 'bully' was a positive term (as in 'bully for you!') and it referred to a 'sweetheart' or 'fine fellow'. (A bit like a great stud bull!) Later the meaning deteriorated to refer to a 'harasser of the weak'.

In recent years, there has been much attention focused on bullying, sometimes to the absurd point where boys are not allowed to rough and tumble at certain schools for fear of being labelled as bullies.

A bully seeks to have power over another child. They may call them names, isolate them, threaten them, damage their property, hurt them (physically or emotionally), or force them to do things which they do not want to. The bully, by doing some or any of these things, makes the other child feel afraid.

Bullies do this as a way to boost themselves. They like to be seen as popular and 'the boss'. It is their feeling of inadequacy that makes the practice so appealing. Naturally, they will pick on weaker or insecure children, children who are different in some way, or who have not learnt to stand up for themselves. Such children offer less resistance. Perhaps the bully may have experienced bullying him/herself, either through a sibling or parent, and has now learnt that behaviour as a way to rule the roost. In consequence, they may not feel that what they are doing is wrong. After all, if Dad hits and abuses Mum, why should the child respond in any other way at school?

The victim can end up feeling isolated, insecure, lacking in self-esteem, inadequate and different from other children – all of which affects their ability to integrate with their peers. The effects can be long-term, which is why bullying is so dangerous. Other children who have complied with the bully and not stood up for their friends may also experience guilt. Sadly, the victim of bullying can easily turn into the perpetrator, if the habit is not dealt with correctly.

Signs that your child may be the victim of a habitual bully include insomnia, anxiety, a drop in school results, moodiness, withdrawal, not wanting to go to school, aggression to siblings, bruises etc. Often children are afraid to tell their parents about what is happening.[1]

Bullies have low self-esteem and often come from backgrounds with parents who have similar issues. Belittled and often abused or witnesses to abuse, they soon learn a dog-eats-dog approach to life. Often, the parents are not open to the idea that the problem really starts at home and so, no matter how much counselling the school offers to the child, the root cause remains. It is a sad and traumatic situation for all concerned.

The victim, however, who like the bully may also suffer from low self-esteem, can be taught to stand up for him/her self, as well as encouraged to form bonds with other children who may be feeling isolated as well. In unity, there is strength.

Constantly needing to go to the toilet

Like bed-wetting, urinating frequently (provided all physical infections etc. have been ruled out) relates to fear and anxiety. It usually occurs outside the home environment, when the child may be afraid or feel insecure. By relieving him or herself, a certain amount of the fear and tension is released. For a parent stuck with a full shopping trolley, in the middle of a shopping centre, it can be exasperating and *piss you off!* However, expressing this anger may only add to a child's anxiety and exacerbate the problem.

If it happens at school, it may indicate that the child is afraid or anxious about something or someone. The bladder stores and releases the body's toxins. Like a balloon, it is able to expand and contract to hold a fairly large quantity of urine. When it cannot accommodate a small amount of urine without needing to release it, it is an indication that the child is having difficulty in adapting to changes in their life. They can't contain the new experience and release it prematurely. Emotional pressure becomes physical pressure, which the child needs to release. The child can also use the need to find a toilet to manipulate a situation as a leverage of power. When little or no urine is passed, it is an indication of the child's inability to release the emotions that have built up.

Sometimes it occurs when there is just too much happening for the child to come to terms with and, like the bladder, the child cannot take the pressure of the situation and so wants to release it as soon as possible. Our children lead very busy lives – far busier than the life I can recall I lived as a child. There are so many extra-murals, classes and events that it is not surprising when a child, particularly a sensitive child, finds it hard and scary to contain. No wonder they want to get it out of their system, and quickly!

Defecating problems

'My child was perfectly potty-trained until we went to in-laws on holiday. There, whilst he controlled his bladder perfectly, he defecated frequently in his trousers. Why?'

We refer to someone as 'anal', or 'anally retentive', when we mean that they can't let go and enjoy life as they are so busy holding on to issues, usually material. Through the anus, we can control when and how we let go of our stuff. So, emotionally, defecating relates to issues of control. When we feel the need to control, it is because we do not trust the world in which we live. By attempting to control others, we make our world feel safer.

Children have few ways of controlling their environment. The only options are to refuse certain foods or to release inappropriately. They also realize that this can cause an inconvenience for their parents and, in being the cause of this problem, they feel in some way empowered. It can result from being forced to spend hours on a potty. By soiling themselves, they can express their anger at parental domination. Sometimes, it can reflect the parents' habit of *dumping their own shit* or negative emotional issues inappropriately. *Giving you shit* is the only tool left to the child to show defiance. Refusing to let go, on the other hand, is also a sign of not wanting to release their control, usually to a parental figure.

In the case of the child mentioned above, he no doubt resented the intrusion of relatives into his time with his parents. He may also have picked up the emotional *shit*, which was occurring between the various in-laws. The strange environment and people may also have made him afraid. *Shitting himself* was his way of releasing these fears as well as making him feel more in control of the situation.

Toilet training involves learning to control muscles that have previously acted spontaneously. The child usually has no particular desire to master these skills and so the development of them becomes a battleground of wills between child and parent. In learning when to hold on and let go, a pattern is established for life, both on an emotional and physical level.

The worst case I have encountered – of the opposite problem: refusing to defecate – was that of a three-year-old who accompanied her parents and sibling on an exotic island holiday. The destination reached, the child was placed in the Kiddies Care Club while the parents took some time out and went sightseeing. For a small, fragile child to have been totally removed from her familiar environment and placed in the care of complete strangers must have been terrifying. In her defiance, fear and insecurity, she chose to attempt to exert what little control she had, by refusing to defecate. She needed to hold on to the familiar. The seven day holiday ended and she still had refused to let go. Consequently, she was forced to go to hospital and have an enema.

While understandable from a health point of view, from the child's perspective, her needs had once again been subjugated. This set up a continuous battle of wills as, from then on, the child developed the habit of refusing to let go, resulting in regular trips to the hospital for enemas. Psychologist and author, Anodea Judith, says, *Repeated use of enema is tantamount to sexual abuse, only the abuse is to the first chakra rather than the second chakra of sexuality (though in some cases it may have sexual overtones). This invasion of the area most closely related to the root chakra destroys the trust so crucial at this stage, and literally fractures one's sense of solidity. Difficulty with boundaries is guaranteed, creating either impenetrable walls or non-existent boundaries. The first chakra right to have is denied, as the child's only solid creation is taken away against her will at a time out of sync with the body. In reaction, energy is pulled upwards toward the head, resulting in either an inability to hold and contain or an excessive need to do so, as well as a damaged sense of autonomy (a third chakra issue).*[2] A less invasive way of dealing with the problem may have resolved the issue without the need for repeated enemas and their long-term emotional effects.

In refusing to release the contents of their bowels, the child attempts to exert their control or will against authority figures. As they physically hold on to their faeces, they hold on to their power. The matter needs to be dealt with sensitively and perhaps an area of empowerment created for the child, so that they can transfer this need on to something less damaging to their health. Harsh discipline only drives the need deeper; the desire to rebel increases. Trust in the world and authority figures is an issue that needs to be established, if the child is going to feel safe to let go with ease.

Farting

Most kids (and some adults) enjoy farting. It's a way of *letting off steam;* consequently, we feel better for it afterwards. Everyone does it to the tune of about one and half litres of gas daily. It's more of a universal body function than a habit. Boys take exceptional delight in farting *(it's a gas!)* because, in some ways, it is an act of aggression. By leaving a foul odour in the air, we *create a stink* for everyone else to deal with. In this context it shows a desire for dominance in the pack. Just as in pack animals when an alpha male sprays his territory with urine, the smell indicates to others who rules the roost (or who would like to).

Head-banging

Does your child move his or her head rhythmically against a solid object, most often just before sleeping or when he or she is upset? Many young children (up to 20%) bang their heads. Boys are three times more likely than girls to develop this habit which, while causing their parents concern, is rarely damaging. It unusually develops around six months and stops between the ages of two and three although, in some cases, it may continue for longer. In some instances, it may be an indication of developmental problems or autism.[3]

Although this is not necessarily the case, it is worth taking your child to a paediatrician for an examination to alleviate any concern, particularly if he or she is still head-banging past the age of three and if he or she is not interacting with you or has developmental delays.

Head-rolling or body-rolling is similar to head-banging. It seems the infant derives pleasure and comfort from the habit, which may relate to the movement they experienced *in utero* and being rocked to sleep. There may also be a link to the vestibular of the inner ear which controls balance and gets stimulated by this movement. Typically, toddlers do not injure themselves while performing this habit. They are as yet too small to generate sufficient force to cause brain damage. Obviously, the risk increases as they get older; this is one of the reasons why it is more of a cause for concern in older children.

Sometimes head-banging can be an attempt to gain attention, particularly if combined with a tantrum. The greater the reaction, the more the habit will continue. It can also be a sign of boredom, frustration and a way of releasing tension – or have you not heard of *banging your head against a brick wall?* Some of this tension may be within the child or within the environment. Over- or under-stimulated infants are also subject to this habit.

As they get older, children develop other ways to achieve the same result, through swings, dancing, bumping each other, jumping ropes etc. In older children, head-banging can be a sign of anger at not being heard or understood, confusion and internalized aggression.

Interrupting

You're trying to put together a major business deal or your close friend is about to reveal a juicy piece of gossip and you can't hear a word because your two-year-old has jumped on your lap and is jabbering away at the top of his/her voice while pulling your hair. Whenever you are in mid-sentence, your toddler interrupts you – whether you are on the phone or talking to a friend. The behaviour is relentless and no amount of attempts at diversion seems to be successful. This *butting in,* as with the billy goat from which the phrase derives, is a stubborn attempt to gain control and the attention of the parent or situation. It can be most annoying to both the listener and the speaker.

Interrupting is an indicator that boundary issues are not in place, particularly in an older child. They are unsure as to where they end and where you begin. Through their insecurity, they constantly attempt to gain control of you and the conversation. By allowing children to invade your boundaries, you can create greater insecurity as there doesn't feel as if there is a safe container for their expression. A calm, but firm 'not now' creates a boundary for both of you. When your conversation is complete, you can then turn to the child and give them the **full** focus of your attention. Without boundaries, a child will feel insecure. However, excessive boundaries will have the same effect. As a parent, a balance needs to be achieved for the child to feel safe and yet not completely constricted.

Nose-picking

(See also page 113)

It's not uncommon to see a child or an adult (often whilst driving!) having a good old dig for treasure bogeys! Our noses represent recognition. When our nasal passages are constantly blocked, we express a thwarted desire to be recognized. We then constantly try to remove the blockages, in the form of snot. Snot is a mixture of mucus and dust. Mucus represents congealed feelings and hardened tears. If yellow, these backed-up feelings may have become infected or toxic. It is our unshed tears which combine with dirt and *get up our nose.* A child who makes a habit of picking his or her nose is indicating that, on some level, they want to breathe freely and clear out unwanted stuck issues. The desire for recognition may be creating self-imposed obstacles or difficulties, so they set about removing the *sticky business.* As for eating the result…!

An old wives' tale says that children who nose-pick may have worms. Therefore, it might be time for a 'clear out', emotionally and physically, of what is eating away at the child. Perhaps a check-up for worms is worth a try – consult your GP. Maybe the old wives had a point!

Tantrums

Few mothers don't have a horror of their two-year-old rolling on the floor and screaming blue murder in the middle of a shopping centre on a busy Saturday morning, particularly when passers-by glare at the mother, nod their heads and say, 'poor child'. Those minutes can seem like hours as your toddler shows no sign of stopping the racket and you feel increasingly helpless.

Actually, in spite of being called the 'terrible twos', tantrums can start before two years of age and continue a lot longer. (Or haven't you seen an adult *throw his/her toys out of the cot* when things don't work out the way he/she wanted?) Tantrums are a normal part of a child's development and, just as different children have different natures, so the degree and frequency of tantrums will differ from child to child.

I don't care how many times books tell you to see tantrums as 'opportunities for education'; the fact is that education is usually the last thing on a stressed-out parent's mind as their offspring yells the shopping-centre down. Tantrums commonly concern opposition and frustration. The child wants what it can't have. It has chosen something and its choice is being thwarted. As adults, most of us have learnt to control our anger at having our choice squashed (such as when one partner dominates the TV remote) without sulking or throwing a tantrum. However, a toddler has not yet learnt to deal with desire and refusal. Sometimes the frustration at not being able to manipulate the world becomes too much too contain. The problem is exacerbated when the child is tired, hungry or unwell.

At this age, children may also battle to make up their minds. They may think they want something only to change their minds when it arrives. This causes them and the parents further frustration. As the child starts to leave its mother's side, he or she learns that they are separate entities from the mother. The child also learns that he or she has a will that may differ from the mother's. When the mother doesn't comply with the child's will, for a child who has just learnt to communicate verbally, it can feel like discussing the finer points of Renaissance architecture with a sheep. They just don't seem to get what it is that you want. To someone who is just developing a will of their own, the resulting frustration is huge.

Tantrums may manifest as the desire to have willpower over someone else – to let their will win. If they lose, they feel powerless. If they win, then they only have to yell the place down again to win the war. Too much discipline and the child's will may get broken, independent action is reduced and self-esteem will suffer. Too little, and the child believes that they are omnipotent (i.e. a precocious brat). Take a balanced, calm approach and the child will develop individuality and healthy self-esteem.

Giving in to your child is a recipe for further tantrums. It's the easiest of the options but potentially the most damaging. Offering minor choices is one way of avoiding a tantrum, as in: 'do you want apple or litchi juice?' By empowering the child to make a choice, you are fulfilling their need for independence. Don't take the child out when they are tired, unwell or hungry. In the throws of a tantrum, reflect back to the child what is disturbing him/her. Just knowing that you understand can help to calm things down. Often a gentle hug helps. Try not to lose your temper, as the two of you screaming only exacerbates the problem. Spanking doesn't help either, as you simply teach the child that violence is an okay way to behave. By demonstrating calmness yourself, you set an example to the child of what behaviour you expect. Children mimic their parents. A school-age child can be sent to his/her room to cool off.

Why do some children throw more tantrums than others and continue to have tantrums past the toddler age? This can be due to having a stronger will, a more fiery nature, success in getting their way with past tantrums, watching their parents scream and shout and so learning that this as an acceptable way to behave, repressed anger, low self-esteem, very authoritarian/dominating parents or undisciplined parents with few boundaries.

Tantrums are a normal part of development but, like anything in life, when they are excessive, they indicate that something in the psyche of the child or its environment is out of balance.

Endnotes

1 Bullying: Bullying Online www.bullying.co.uk

2 Psychologist and author Judith, Anodea, p.74, *Eastern Body Western Mind*, Celestial Arts, Berkeley, California, 1996.

3 Head-banging: drgreene.com by Allan Greene MD, and Child Symptoms: Rocking/Head-banging www.aap.org/pubserv/rocking.htm AAP.

Chapter Twelve
Better late than never

Procrastination and Punctuality

Procrastination

Procrastination is the grave in which opportunity is buried.

Author Unknown

'Stop nagging me, I'll do it.' How many of us have said that at some stage in our lives, only to remember a week later that we still haven't done what was required? How often haven't you had a pile of work to do and found yourself chatting about the soccer results for ages with a colleague? When you have a critical deadline looming, do you find yourself lolling in front of the TV, watching the third re-run of *How Clean is Your House?*

Procrastination is almost endemic amongst the human race, with one in five people being classified as chronic procrastinators. The advent of the internet has provided procrastinators with an even better way to while away the hours rather than do the job that needs to be done. It's so much more fun to check your emails, go gaming, view a few web pages, enrol in yet another online dating service or head for the chat room. Rather than increase our productivity, research by Tim Pychyl and his assistant Jennifer Lavoie of Carleton University, discovered that 47% of the time we spend online is to avoid actually working.[1] That is a huge dent in the work life of an average employee.

Time management and procrastination are not as closely related as one might assume. The majority of procrastinators are well aware of what they should be doing, even while they play yet another round of PlayStation. Then, why do procrastinators procrastinate?

Low-self-esteem is the most significant of a procrastinator's traits; it is disguised in any number of ways. Where there is low self-esteem, there is inevitably a large ego. Why? Because in order to compensate for feelings of inadequacy, we need to inflate ourselves. To do so, our ego creates a world where it can thrive, at the expense of our higher selves. That's not to say that low self-esteem is specific to procrastinators. Most of us suffer from low self-esteem in some area or another – be it our bodies, our achievements, our lack of qualifications, our lack breeding or failed relationships. With procrastination, however, many of the attributes of low self-esteem, (as opposed to just a few in other behaviour) are involved.

Our lower self, rather than our higher self, prevails in procrastination in the form of:

- false optimism and self-deception – seeing things as we would like them to be rather than as they are
- enjoying the panic – crisis management
- believing we need to be perfect
- fear of failure
- blame
- feeling a victim / self-pity
- attempting to control and manipulate others / the need for power
- feeling guilty for not doing what we know we should – both past and present
- believing we don't have the time – we are 'too busy'
- believing that the task is too inferior for us / believing that we are inferior to the task
- stubbornness
- lack of skill or knowledge / scale of task
- boredom
- passive resistance
- needing to please others – taking on more than we can do
- resisting change

Reasons for procrastination

Optimism is often part of the problem. The procrastinator believes that he or she will meet the required deadline and lulls him/herself and colleagues into a false sense of security. Time creeps by, before he or she finally realizes that there is not enough time left to complete the project.

Crisis management: Enjoy base-jumping? Climbed Mount Everest and K2 without oxygen? Do you have a need to skydive? Then maybe, just maybe, you are addicted to thrill-seeking – only life has put you in a small study where you are required to write a detailed thesis on the nocturnal habits of the aardvark. What better way, then, to express your real thrill-seeking desires than by failing to do anything about the thesis until the night before it is due to be handed in? After all, if you can pull this one off, bungee-jumping from the statue of liberty should present no problem! Maybe, you actually enjoy the challenge of the *panic*. A career in dentistry, specializing in the treatment of under fives with behavioural problems, should work for you!

This is where the wheels start to come off, as the procrastinator pacifies him/her self with phrases such as 'I work best under pressure' or 'when the going gets tough, the tough get going'.

When I worked for a large, international advertising agency, I would see this pattern repeated time and time again. The Creative Director would do little about a briefing for a job until closing time on the day before the presentation. Then there was a sudden wild flurry of activity long into the night, before a campaign was thrown together, causing considerable stress and a debatable standard of work. The following day, exhausted, everyone would head off to the pub to celebrate the completion of the campaign, while other jobs' deadlines hung like thunderclouds overhead.

Surprisingly, the campaign would often meet with success, while we would be cynical about the clients' ability to detect our lack of input into it. With acceptance came the reinforcement that this approach worked, and so there was little requirement to alter this 'crisis management' way of working. For the Creative Director, there was the high of having battled against the odds and won through, which in itself becomes fairly addictive – we need the rush and the high and the sense of achievement. It boosts our egos.

Closely linked to optimism, **self-deception** thrives amongst procrastinators. Being an extension of our ego, we will seldom admit to being procrastinators – instead, we will always find a perfectly justifiable excuse as to why we have not completed the said task. We live in an illusionary world, which we maintain with phrases such as 'I thrive under pressure', 'if you can't do it perfectly then don't do it at all', 'there's too much else on my plate', 'I need to clear my thinking before I start,' or 'it's not fair that I should have to do this', amongst others.

To overcome self-deception and false optimism, we need to look at ourselves long and hard in an emotional mirror. Ask yourself why you delay in completing tasks. Then write a rebuttal next to each of your replies. Be honest with yourself. It may feel uncomfortable but that is part of the process.

Our ego, then, demands extremely high standards of us and we doubt our ability to produce them; we remain like scared hedgehogs, in little balls, refusing to move. The ego wants **perfectionism** – except that the ego is both judge and jury and, consequently, no matter what we produce, it will always judge the result as inadequate. Rather than have to face this demon of our own making, we avoid the task. To resolve perfectionist issues, we need to realize that that there is nothing in the universe that can be classified as perfect, as each person's judgement of perfection differs. Some men like Posh, some like Britney, some don't rate either of them. For something to be perfect it must be complete. Nothing in the universe is actually complete. When we die our life may be over and yet, in a sense, we live on. A day dies but is reborn twelve hours later. To seek perfection is to seek an illusion, for either everything is perfect or nothing is.

Waiting to start a project for fear of its not being perfect, then, is waiting for something that can never be. After I wrote my last book, there was so much more I wanted to add after it had been published. That's how it is: everything is a work in progress. Usually, a desire for perfection is simply a mask for a lack of self-confidence.

A friend had a husband who would take simply ages to write the simplest of letters – for instance, to the plumber, querying a bill. He would be up all night trying to get the wording just right, only to collapse in a heap of scrunched paper with the letter still not having been written.

Remember that fear always lurks behind perfectionism. Confronting your fears and allowing yourself the right to be human can, paradoxically, make you a far happier and more productive person.[2] Dr. David M. Burns

We are also **afraid of failure.** Not wanting to admit this, the ego or lower self launches a scathing attack on all those whom we perceive are to blame for our inability to complete a task. We feel a victim of circumstances or of others' demands, as in 'how could he only give me two weeks in which to complete this task?' 'My not starting it is actually his fault.' 'She does not understand the complexity of what is involved.' 'They just don't understand that I need time to think the job through.' 'I always get picked for the worst jobs.' Rather than look inward, we search outwardly for a reason why we haven't done the task, and indulge in self-pity for the unfortunate situation that has been thrust upon us. Our fear of failure also causes us to resist starting a project, as to do so may involve failing. Rather than confront this reality, we procrastinate.

We excel at minimizing our achievements and, when a situation has the potential to take us out of our victim status to that of a victor, we sabotage it: 'I knew all along that they were out to get me, so it didn't seem worth completing the report, although they offered me a promotion to do so'. This is typical of how we shoot ourselves in the foot. Ask yourself why it is so scary for you to be powerful or successful. Do you feel you may be rejected if success comes your way? Were you constantly told as a child that you were not good enough? Perhaps answering these questions may help you to understand why you would prefer to fail than to succeed.

What better way to **control and manipulate** others than by deliberately delaying the start of a project. This works particularly well in group or team situations where your role is key to the outcome. Simply sit back and do nothing, while watching the stress levels of those around you rise. It's a sure fire way to feed your ego by making everyone realize just how much they need you and how important you are to the project.

This was wonderfully demonstrated during a corporate art workshop I was giving. Each team had to paint a portrait of themselves on one large sheet of paper. Time was limited to five minutes per group. One participant, who clearly had self-esteem issues, took the paintbrush first, taking ages to paint herself at the expense of the rest of the team, a couple of whom did not get to paint at all in the allotted time. In discussions after the exercise, it became clear that this was a pattern that was present in the workplace and which was the cause of much anger and frustration amongst her colleagues. While she delayed completing her task of typing up the briefs required for her colleagues to proceed, she used up valuable time which her colleagues had to make up by working late and/or missing their deadlines. Not being at the end of the task, she missed the firing line when management did not receive work to deadline. So, she continued to wield a huge amount of manipulative power, which other felt helpless to do anything about.

Feeling **guilty** for letting others down or for not meeting deadlines can become a good place to wallow if we choose to. Rather than move on to the next project and achieve better timing there, we make our guilt an excuse for not starting something. 'I feel so bad for letting everyone down.' We are bad: they are good. We live so polarized an existence that we become afraid to move for fear of repeating the experience. Any pleasure is taken out of the new challenge as, ridden with past guilt, we feel compelled to hold ourselves back from enjoying the new task as a punishment. Work not enjoyed holds little enticement, so we resist the process, telling ourselves things like, 'this is all I really deserve.'

Feeling deflated, our ego grasps at ways to inflate who we are. What better way, then, than to be so much in demand that we simply have no time to be concerned with the minor demands of deadline: 'I am so **busy** working on plans for the proposed reorganization of the company, that your small requirements for me actually to do the tasks I was employed to do are superfluous.' 'If I wait till just before it's due, then I won't waste so much time on it.' We create *busyness* in our *business,* often over-inflating our role and importance and justifying at length why we are so busy, all of which time could have been spent working.

Our ego may lead us to believe that the task we have been asked to do is too **inferior** for us. Therefore, rather than actually do it, which would be belittling for a person in our position, we avoid doing it. If we were to do it and fail, then we would have to confront our own inadequacies which we have tried so hard to conceal. The other side of this coin is the belief that we are inferior and therefore destined to fail in the allotted task, such as 'Every time I try something new, I fail.' Naturally, we will resist trying anything new.

Stubbornness is another way of building up resistance to doing the job. When we feel small, we resist others who appear to push us around. 'I need to be in the right space to do this job and I'm not in that space now, so I'm not going to do it.' 'What right has he/she to tell *me* what to do?' 'Relax, stop getting hassled; it's not the end of the world if it doesn't happen.' By not complying, we demonstrate to the other person that we are not someone who can be pushed into submission. Try asking your nine-year-old to tidy his/her room and you may well be met with this reaction.

Often, fearing that we lack the required *skills or knowledge* for a task can be a determining factor in causing us to procrastinate. If angels fear to tread, then only fools would rush in to start such a task. Better delay the process and hopefully the angels may just take it away! We have also been brought up to believe that, before we do anything, whether it's art or baking, we need to have done some sort of course or degree. Only then will we have the required skills. As a child, this was learnt behaviour: 'You can't pass until you have studied and written exams.' We still carry this concept over into adulthood and it frequently holds us back from initiating anything.

Carolyn Myss, author, metaphysical teacher and medical intuitive, says *If you have the inspiration, you have the talent.*[3] This block over lack of skills is a huge inhibitor when it comes to making a concept a reality. Many worthy dreams are never fulfilled because of it. One person I admired put it like this: Find what you are most afraid of doing and then do it. By doing so, we grow in leaps and bounds, and so does our self-esteem.

Sometimes, in our enthusiasm we create an **enormous task** for ourselves to complete, as in 'next month I'll have lost 10 stone, stopped smoking and drinking and be attending the gym at least 6 times a week.' The idea is great, the scale of it daunting; naturally, we procrastinate in doing it, months turn into years and still we smoke, drink and look like a beached whale. Were we to take one small aspect of the task ahead and complete that, the sense of self-worth achieved would give a greater drive to achieving the next small task and so on. So we could, for instance, agree to drinking only two glasses of beer a night and cutting out cream from our diet. Each task we complete builds the self-esteem which enables us to achieve the following task we set ourselves. Here is a chart to demonstrate this:

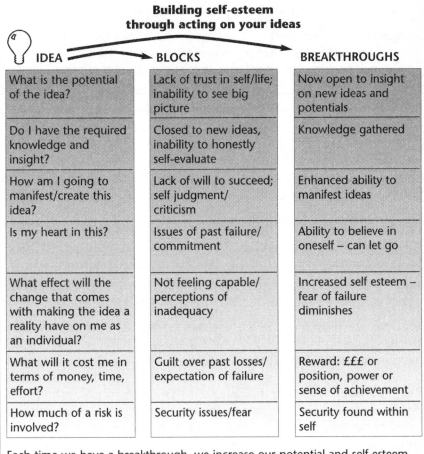

Building self-esteem through acting on your ideas

IDEA	BLOCKS	BREAKTHROUGHS
What is the potential of the idea?	Lack of trust in self/life; inability to see big picture	Now open to insight on new ideas and potentials
Do I have the required knowledge and insight?	Closed to new ideas, inability to honestly self-evaluate	Knowledge gathered
How am I going to manifest/create this idea?	Lack of will to succeed; self judgment/ criticism	Enhanced ability to manifest ideas
Is my heart in this?	Issues of past failure/ commitment	Ability to believe in oneself – can let go
What effect will the change that comes with making the idea a reality have on me as an individual?	Not feeling capable/ perceptions of inadequacy	Increased self esteem – fear of failure diminishes
What will it cost me in terms of money, time, effort?	Guilt over past losses/ expectation of failure	Reward: £££ or position, power or sense of achievement
How much of a risk is involved?	Security issues/fear	Security found within self

Each time we have a breakthrough, we increase our potential and self-esteem even if the idea does not materialise in the way we had initially planned.
Each time we stop ourselves from going beyond the block, we reduce our future ability and potential to explore new ideas.

There are simply some tasks in the world that are **boring.** I have just collected the dog do from the garden and hung up the washing. Not exactly exhilarating tasks, particularly as the dog had eaten seaweed which had done something strange to his digestion! Now, it's natural to want to delay the tasks for as long as is hygienically possible, yet boredom can be an approach we *choose* to take in life. It's all a matter of how we approach a project. There can be a huge amount of satisfaction in getting things done, even if the excitement/challenge level was zero. Often, if we list the tasks to do, we are quite happy to take on the tasks at the lower end of the list, if only to avoid the ones at the top end. By manipulating this natural preference, we can still get a whole lot of tasks completed, if not all of them. For instance, picking up dog do did not get this book completed, but it was useful, provided a break from writing, and the reward of feeling that something had been completed.

In the previously-mentioned BBC programme, *How Clean is Your House?*, many of the participants simply procrastinate until the task of cleaning their homes becomes so enormous, that many of them confess that they don't know where to begin. This is where adapting the small-steps policy helps.

Passive resistance:

'Put the dog out, honey.'

'Mmm,' says he, engrossed in the *Telegraph*, whilst idly fondling the remote.

'Honey, I asked you to let Tiddles out.'

'Yes, yes, I'll do it.'

Still Tiddles remains indoors. A further twenty minutes pass. Tension and anger in the room has risen considerably. 'Henry, I'm trying to get supper cooked; let the dog out before he messes in the house.'

Meet passive resistance. When we don't want to confront someone directly about how they undermine our sense of self – or when we feel that they are more important, confident etc. than we are – we are afraid to say 'no' outright. So we procrastinate over doing what they require of us, as a way of resisting their authority. Deep down we are angry, yet unable to express and, in some cases, even connect with that anger, so we sabotage their wishes. It's the only way we feel we can stand up to them.

We may be angry or resentful towards someone so that delaying a project is a subconscious way of getting even with them.

Learning to say 'no' is a boundary issue that few of us seem to have acquired. Hence, we open ourselves up to accepting more and more work which we have little hope of completing. Yet this seems easier than a simple 'no'. This is also an issue born of low self-esteem; we want to please or gain others' approval. We feel guilty saying no. By doing so, we put ourselves under enormous pressure and stress as we can't complete all of the tasks on hand and so resist starting, often as a passive-aggressive way of getting back at those who have pressurized us in the first place.

What would happen if we were to complete a long and arduous task successfully, for instance? Why, we might gain promotion, empowerment, recognition or any other positive result, which would probably result in change. So we sabotage the outcome by refusing to complete the task. Not because we can't do it, but because completion equals change and, for us humans, change is as popular as climbing Everest in Gucci stilettos.

We can't move into a new future if we still have so much to do today. So our **resistance to change** actually has very noble reasons attached to it, such as: 'Yes, I know I've been promising to do such and such, but I'm so snowed under I can't think of doing it now.' We have to change if we are to grow emotionally, mentally and spiritually, yet we procrastinate doing so with every part of ourselves and create more baggage to hold us back. This is also reflected in the other ailments of which chronic procrastinators have a higher incidence than normal. These include insomnia, poor diet, digestive problems, colds, as well as higher levels of depression and low self-esteem.[4]

How we procrastinate falls into three categories: physical, emotional and mental. So we may physically procrastinate by going for a walk, sleeping or going to a movie. We can emotionally procrastinate by escaping into alcohol, drugs, reading trashy magazines or flirting to escape from the reality of the task at hand. Mentally, we might create a number or reasons why we should not do the job, such as *maybe I need to get some more eggs from the shops now, or I need to find inspiration, or I'll start tomorrow.*

To **stop procrastinating** you are going to have to:

1. Be **honest** about the fact that you are procrastinating.
2. Write down the **reasons** (from the list earlier in this chapter) why you are procrastinating.
3. **Challenge** these reasons. Don't let yourself off lightly. To overcome a low self-esteem issue takes discipline. Realize that it is your ego

talking when you say 'I'll do it tomorrow,' or 'I need to have fun/relax/smoke/have coffee first.' The ego is hedonistic – don't let it rule!

4. Write down the **consequences** of not doing the task on time.
5. Break the task down into bite-sized chunks / **set realistic goals**.
6. **Start** the task.
7. **Affirm** your action positively.
8. **Remember that success breeds success!**

Punctuality

Do your friends invite you to dinner an hour earlier than everyone else because they count on your being late? Do you have numerous letters from your employer threatening you with dismissal for being late? Or are you the sort of person who, in your keenness to be on time, ends up confronting the hostess dripping wet and with a towel wrapped around her assuring you that it's fine that you are a 'few minutes early'?

Different cultures have totally different concepts of time. In Germany, to be late is to cause great offence to your hosts, whereas in Latin America you would be an oddity if you arrived punctually.

Social psychologists ascribe the differences in perspectives on time to the cultural, religious and personality traits of various cultures. There is even a theory which says that those further away from the equator have to be more careful with the timing of planting their crops than do those who live closer to the equator: if you plant too early or too late, snow or frost could eradicate your entire crop. This, then, is the reason given for Mediterranean people's putting less emphasis on time than do their more northern counterparts.

Punctuality, or lack of it, is also catching. It only takes one person to be consistently late for a meeting and, in time, others will put less importance on being on time. This principal was used in Ecuador, where everyone synchronized their watches as part of a national campaign aimed at instilling an ethic of time-keeping in the population. Chronic lateness had, according to a study, cost Ecuador $2.5 billion a year, a sizeable amount for a country with a gross domestic product of $24 billion.[5]

Being late has also become associated with control and power. No self-respecting diva would make an entrance on time! The word 'punctual' comes from the Latin word *punctualis*, which itself derives from *punctum,* which means a 'point' or 'pricking'. If we arrive late, do we *miss the point?* When we are punctual we *get the point.* If we are always late or behind, we need to examine what is behind our behaviour. For someone who has walked down the aisle after the bride on one too many occasions, this behaviour pushes my buttons!

Just as procrastination mirrors a lack of self-worth, so does not being punctual. This lack of self-worth affects our integrity, such that what we say is not necessarily what we *do*. Because we feel inadequate, we seek to boost ourselves by attempting to appear important. What better way to manipulate others than by having them wait and waste their time while we occupy ourselves in more important other ways?

There are, however, different archetypal categories of latecomer, from which you may be able to identify yourself. They are listed below:

- Ego-tripper
- Diva
- Busy-ness person
- Passive resister
- Space cadet

Archetypes and punctuality

When we feel less, we have to make ourselves feel more. Our **ego** loves this role and creates wonderful situations for us to trip ourselves up. We feel that, as part of our esteemed role in life, it is fine to make others wait for our arrival. Their time is, after all, not as valuable as ours. If they are not aware of this fact, then we will ensure that they are, by being late! This feels quite acceptable to us, whether we are dealing with a friend or colleague.

The **diva** is closely related to the ego-tripper in that, due to their 'stardom' – be it on account of their being the niece of the CEO or a celebrity in their own right – they have the right to 'make an entrance'. They may have been ready ages before, but careful timing will ensure a theatrical entrance that no-one could possibly miss.

The **busy-ness** person is just that. They believe that, by seeming to be constantly rushing, they appear not only to be working hard, but also of great value to any company. Often, the busy-ness is a mask for their inability to actually do the job. If they are busy, they must be good. Busy-ness can also be a genuine result of taking on too many responsibilities or tasks with little hope of completing them. We say, 'I have to drive to so and so. Well, in that case, I'll just stop in at X's and drop off something, then while I'm there it would make sense to go to the post office and I'd better pay the electricity at the same time.' Before you know it, a simple trip becomes one fraught with tension as you try to fit everything in and in so doing become later and later for the actual appointment. Sometimes, this comes about from wanting to be constantly busy so that we don't have to face what is actually important in our lives. By keeping so busy, the less comfortable, emotional concerns are kept at bay. It can also result from a belief that no one else is quite as capable as we are at doing the task, which is the other side of the self-esteem coin.

The **passive resister** does not actually want to be doing what he or she has committed to do. Being late is a way of resisting in a non-confrontational, non-verbal manner, what we would rather avoid. Let's say Aunt Mabel has invited you to tea with the family. Now, the last time you had the pleasure, she and your cousins spent the entire afternoon pointedly enquiring as to when you were going to marry and get a 'proper' job. Needless to say, you are not keen to go to this occasion and so finding things that need doing is a way of saying, 'I'll come but under my terms.'

The **space cadet** is so busy devising new theories of relativity or unique art happenings that time is not relative. Our cadet is so busy floating in the realms of conceptual thinking that touchdown doesn't occur. Hence, its not that they are late as such, just that time, as we understand it, does not exist for them and therefore it's not possible to be late (or early). One simply is, whenever one arrives.

The early arriver

> Better three hours too soon than a minute too late.
>
> William Shakespeare,
> The Merry Wives of Windsor, Act 2, Scene 2

Don't you just hate it? The cashew nut creation has burnt beyond recognition, the cat's eating the mousse, the baby has smeared baby-food all over your outfit and your other half is yelling about having no clean shirts, when the doorbell rings. Tra ra! Your first guest has arrived, a mere fifteen vital minutes early! Now you have to appear quite calm and relaxed, as if smeared baby-food is the mark of any true chef, muttering, 'no, of course it's not inconvenient.'

So why do people arrive early? Like the late arriver, this also has to do with matters of low self-esteem and control. By arriving early, we gain a territorial advantage. We stake out the turf and decide on our patch in order to feel more secure. By arriving early, we are symbolically not being in present time. Whereas the late arriver wants to escape into the future, we hang on to the past. Anxiety about being late is also about not wanting to offend others. In arriving early, we do the very thing that we sought not to do.

Be in your integrity and own honour code, which means arriving at the appointed time. If you are early, go for a short walk. Being on time shows respect for the process or person you are visiting. If you do not show them this, how can you expect to have a respectful relationship?

Endnotes

1 'Having spent some time in university computer labs, where he discovered most students doing anything but what they were supposed to, Pychyl became intrigued by the effect of the networked computer on productivity. He and a grad student, Jennifer Lavoie, surveyed internet surfers about their online work habits. When they tabulated the results late last year, Pychyl and Lavoie discovered that an amazing forty-seven percent of the time we spend online amounts to work avoidance.' From *Cyberslacking and the Procrastination Superhighway, a Web-based Survey of On-Line Procrastination, Attitudes and Emotion* by Jennifer A.A. Lavoie, Simon Fraser University, and Timothy A. Pychyl, Carleton University, 2001, Sage Publications.

2 Dr. David M. Burns author of *Feeling Good: The New Mood Therapy* from www.quotationspage.com

3 Quote from http://myss.com/myss/dailymsgarch.asp

4 'College students who procrastinate in their academic work are also likely to have unhealthy sleep, diet, and exercise patterns, according to one of several studies presented here last week by scholars at the annual meeting of the American Psychological Association.' *Procrastination in College Students is a Marker for Unhealthy Behaviors, Study Indicates* by David Glenn *The Chronicle of Higher Education* 2002 www.physics.ohio-state.edu/-wilkins/writing/Resources/essays/procrastinate.html

5 From the financial page *The New Yorker – Punctuality Pays* by James Surowiecki 2004-03-29.

Chapter Thirteen
The games we play

Manipulative Habits

Whenever we seek to manipulate another person, chances are that it is our fear that drives us to do so. When our world feels out of control and we feel helpless and dis-empowered (afraid), we will attempt to gain power by trying to control and manipulate those around us. The more we get them to do what we want them to do, the more in charge we feel and therefore the less fearful. However, if you are the person being manipulated, the chances are that you'll respond negatively, upsetting your manipulator, who will have to try even harder to bring you back under their control. This is how the cycle continues, until the manipulator or the one being manipulated decides not to play the game anymore. Very often, particularly in an emotionally-dependent relationship, we can play both roles of the manipulator and the manipulated.

Being a game with a minimum of two participants, when one persons recognizes the pattern of what is happening or increases their self-esteem and no longer needs to manipulate, the game simply has to stop.

Let's examine, then, some common ways in which we enjoy manipulating other people.

Lying

Truth is God.

Mahatma Ghandi

In the many talks I have given about habits, lots of people have admitted to a wide variety of habits, from nail-biting to hair twirling, but only one person has had the courage to say 'I lie'. Yet I doubt that there is a person alive who can honestly say that they have never lied, even if only to themselves. 'It's no problem,' when it is, or 'I'll do it tomorrow,' and then you don't, or 'no, there is nothing wrong,' when there is –

these are all part of the web of lies we create, consciously or unconsciously.

It is interesting that there is a dual meaning to the word 'lie'. On the one hand it denotes being horizontal, as in lying down, and on the other to tell an untruth. A link between the two meanings may be seen if we look at the derivation of the word. ' To lie' (as in 'to lie down') is related to the Hittite word *laggari*, which means 'to lie / fall down'. Therefore, when we lie by not being truthful, we 'fall' or 'lie down' spiritually. Doing so slows down our progress. If we go against our conscience, which invariably we do when we lie, we create karma or negative consequences for ourselves. If we sow lies, we will reap untruth.

There 'e go's!

When we lie, most often our egos are in charge. Our egos want us to be seen to be clever, wealthy, important, popular and powerful. If we perceive that the reality of our lives does not match this expectation, then lying becomes a way of fabricating the world our egos want us to inhabit. Eventually, the illusion we have created through our web of lies and reality becomes so intertwined that even we may have trouble differentiating between the two. Lying, then, becomes a way of manipulating others into believing our illusionary world. Children will often do this when they say things like: 'My Dad's the best soccer player ever,' or 'I am a black belt Karate expert.' Neither is true, yet both are what the child *wants* to be true. The more he tells the lie, the more it starts to become the truth – not only for him, but (he hopes) also for those to whom he is telling it.

How we start lying

The habitual liar's habit may start as a small child when, like most children, we rely on our mothers to meet our needs. However, if our mothers, whether through lack of interest or circumstance, do not nurture us, we feel angry. We express this anger by yelling which, if unanswered, leads to sadness and finally to the resignation that our prime nurturer is not able to fulfil our needs. From then on, every time we cry because we are hungry and our cries remain unanswered, rather than face the reality that our mother is not there for us, we simply tell ourselves that we are not really hungry.

Small children will always see themselves as the prime cause for whatever happens in their lives. If mummy is too busy at the office, or daddy runs off with the young blonde from accounts, then the child will most often feel in some way responsible. They may feel that their behaviour is responsible for our not having our needs met, and blame themselves rather than admit that their mother or father is imperfect. Their self-esteem suffers or does not develop, and the lower our self-esteem, the greater our potential for lying.

The line between truth and dishonesty starts to blur and our pattern of lying becomes entrenched, as we seek to rebuild our self-esteem through lies. Being caught up and not assuming responsibility for our lives, we look for someone else to blame. Consequently, we remain victimized by the actions of others because this feels less threatening than confronting our own demons. Even if we are aware of our lying, we will justify our actions by saying, that 'given the circumstances' we had no choice but to fabricate.

Children who are witness to their parents' lying will learn that this is acceptable. So when mum says that she's not going out and then sneaks away, or dad says he'll play ball but sits instead in front of the TV, the child comes to understand not only the feeling of being let down, but also that it is acceptable to do this to others.

Are you living in truth?

Do you lie in order to boost yourself? How well do you trust the process of life? Perhaps you lack trust both in yourself and others? Do you desire to avoid conflict and lie as a consequence? Do you lie to yourself rather than have to change as a consequence of being truthful?

When we live in our truth, we have the ability to manifest what we need in our lives because the centre of truth and manifestation in our bodies is, in the Eastern tradition, the same: i.e. in the throat.

In the Hindu scriptures[1] it is written that those who speak only the truth develop the ability to materialize their words, just as *In the beginning was the word*[2] when God symbolically 'spoke' the world into being.

People who lie compulsively are normally in denial and so do not see that they have a problem. However, if you have had the courage to recognize this pattern within yourself, here are a few suggestions to help you work with it.

Keep a written record of every time you have lied, no matter how small it appeared to be. Then write down next to each lie what you believe your motivation for not being in your truth might have been. Were you motivated by fear? Greed? Inadequacy? Revenge? Desire to boost yourself? Do not judge yourself; simply acknowledge the lie and the motivation behind it. Have compassion for yourself. Then let it go.

Forgive yourself or anyone else concerned and move forward. Keeping this journal will increase your awareness of when you lie and the triggers that lead up to it. Acknowledge that, each time you go against your conscience by lying, you create an imbalance which can only be rectified when you are the recipient of some untruth. So next time someone asks you if their cheque is in the post, just say 'I'm sorry, it's not yet' and thereby lay your karma and conscience (and not your spiritual progress) to rest.

Criticizing

The word 'critical' comes via Latin from the Greek word *krites* meaning 'a judge'. When we are critical of another person, we have chosen to judge or point a finger at them. The old adage of having one finger pointing at another and three fingers pointing back at you comes into play, for it is what we least like in another that is inevitably a mirror of what we don't like about ourselves.

What we dislike in others we dislike in ourselves

The more critical we are of others, the more this is an indication that deep down we dislike ourselves. When you can understand this, it is easier to have compassion for a critical person, as you realize that they are really critical of *themselves*. The people they choose to judge are only mirrors of their own issues. The more we develop ourselves and work through the areas of ourselves which we have come to dislike, the less critical we become of others. However, observing and facing our own emotional issues can be painful and require much courage and, besides, it's so much easier and more fun to pull other people to pieces!

Much harm is done through criticism and many children never achieve their potential, simply because they have been led to believe that they are incapable or useless by over-critical parents or educators.

If you always find yourself accusing others of being stingy, look within yourself to where you may be unable to give. Remember, one's ego is a master of deception. You may believe you are not stingy because you are always giving material goods away to less fortunate people; however, you may be very stingy in giving of yourself emotionally to those close to you.

You could dislike all fat people, seeing them as weak-willed and undisciplined, yet have real issues yourself with food or discipline in other areas of your life. Julia had recovered from bulimia and drug addiction. She was beautiful, tall and slender. She had, though, a huge dislike – to the point of disgust – of anyone who was even slightly overweight. 'I just can't stand even being close to a fat person.' However, two of her clients were particularly large women and she found this a problem. When she could see that their overweight issues mirrored many of her own issues that had led to her bulimia, she came to accept not only them, but herself.

Manipulating with criticism

When we are constantly being criticized by others we start to believe that we are not good enough. Therefore, we work really hard to win affection or love from others, through what we produce and do. Yet the more we try, the less approval we seem to win from these people. We try harder and harder, yet still self-esteem eludes us.

How does one switch off this self-defeating program that reminds us constantly that we are inadequate? If we feel ourselves to be failures, or inadequate, then doing and achieving – no matter how small the task – is a way to start feeling good about ourselves.

What is really happening here is manipulation. In our desire to be loved or approved of, we allow others to pull our strings. The more they withhold approval, the harder we will try to achieve it and the more they will withhold it. Why? Because to do so gives them power. Our power, in fact. Yet we hand it over zealously. We choose to allow them to rule us, in the hope of a moment's approval. Yet doing so remains our choice, so we cannot really blame them.

Whenever we interfere with another person's freewill, we create negative consequences for ourselves. Freewill is what separates us from other life forms. No other animal, mineral or plant species has freewill or choice to the degree that we have. Therefore, when we don't honour another person's decision – even if it is not what we want and try to get them to do what we want them to do – we do not respect their choice. Choice, because it has been bestowed upon each of us, has made us the crown of tangible creation. Therefore, to manipulate with criticism is an act of our lower selves or ego rather than our higher selves. If we want to progress in our development, we will have to work at letting go of the need to make others do what we want them to.

Abuse and the fear of being alone

Abuse in marriage commonly follows this pattern: the more the abuser verbally abuses his/her partner, the less self-worth the partner develops. Consequently, the harder they will try to satisfy their partner's needs which, if the abuser is to remain in power, will never be satisfied. No matter how accommodating one is, it will never be sufficient. No matter how gently one treads, one's steps will always be incorrect. That is what the abuser wants. That is how he/she will manipulate you in order to get you to do what they want. Moreover, the weird thing is that we comply.

Yet research has shown that it is the abuser who most fears being alone, not the person being abused. In spite of their bravado and the seeming worthlessness of the abuser's partner, it is because they are so afraid of being left alone that they abuse. By making their partner feel worthless, they subconsciously believe that their partner will not leave them because they are so useless that no one else would want them; those being abused start believing this. When and if the abused person finally does leave, more often than not it is the abuser who crumbles and the abused person who finds the strength to move on into a new life.

When we belittle others to boost ourselves, we do just that – we want them to *be little*. If they are little and childlike, we can control them like an overbearing parent. When working with the body, one often finds that critical comments have been stored in parts of the body. What happens is that, when I work on an ache or pain, a memory relating to some incident will often come to mind, together with whatever emotion that memory holds. As the person experiences that pain emotionally and is able then to release it, very often the physical symptom goes as well, (albeit in some case it takes a little longer as the physical is grosser and so takes longer to respond).

Jenny suffered from a major ache in her right knee that kept her awake many nights. No apparent reason could be found for her condition, yet the pain continued. Through working with Jenny, it became apparent that her husband felt very threatened by her career success and constantly criticized and belittled her achievements. This made her feel both guilty and frustrated. She wanted to progress but each achievement bore with it the additional upset in her relationship. This pain could also be traced back to similar events in her childhood, where she felt guilty about achieving more than her elder brother (who was in her same class at school) who also did not appreciate his younger sister's achievements and so sought ways to belittle her. Being the right knee, the issue related to men. The knee is an area that we use to move forward in life, as well as being where peer-related issues manifest. It was no surprise, then, that the criticism of others had found its way into Jenny's knee. By working with these issues, we were able to reduce the pain considerably.

Often, these emotions relate to criticism from the past of which the person has no conscious memory. A thoughtless comment carries the potential for huge emotional wounding. If you catch yourself saying something like, 'You stupid child! You'll never learn!', realize that you are writing a program in the mind of that child that will keep repeating day after day, year after year: 'I am stupid and can't ever learn.'

The amplitude with which you say things also plays an important role in imprinting a negative message in someone's brain. Said softly and gently, even the harshest of comments will often have little lasting effect, whereas a simple, 'You're useless,' at top volume and with a huge amount of negative energy attached will carry far more potential damage. Try always to separate the deed from the person, as in: 'What you did was a stupid and dangerous thing and here is why.' Now you have condemned the deed rather than the doer.

Quarrelling

Some people can't seem to help always being at odds with others. They will never miss an opportunity to rise up and attack a person or situation. Yet these people seldom see themselves as the aggressor, rather they view their actions as defensive. No matter how many times they are in a fight, they just don't seem to get that it is they who are really responsible. There is always a constant stream of people or causes that need to be fought. Every day presents opportunities to take offence and to feel justified in retaliating.

It's the neighbour who, instead of simply popping around and asking civilly and calmly if you wouldn't mind stopping your friends from parking across their driveway, will have reported the situation to the police and bad-mouthed you to all and sundry. And when they do come around, they attack you with such ferocity that you are still shaking hours later. From then on, even though you monitor your friends' parking, rude letters, official complaints and threatening phone calls become a daily occurrence for issues as small as your cat crossing their lawn or the smell from your barbeque.

Petra was beside herself with frustration. 'My neighbour keeps tossing these dog turds over the wall into my garden. He claims they are from my dogs going on his front lawn. Any attempt on my part to persuade him otherwise is met with angry recriminations and refusals to believe me. I simply can't speak to the man without him exploding. The final quarrel came when both my dogs had been put down, as they were very old, and still the turds kept coming. I approached him and informed him of my dogs' deaths and told him that this was proof that for all this time my dogs had not been responsible. Instead of apologizing, he simply flew into another torrent of anger regarding my daughters. At this point I gave up, realizing that he simply likes to quarrel.'

It's as if the need to quarrel gives them a reason to live. They become fired up with vitriolic passion which they enjoy spewing in every direction. In spite of the huge waste of energy and time, there are people who derive immense pleasure from a constant quarrel.

When we have an excess of fire or anger within us, it is often an indication that we are really angry with ourselves. We feel impotent to really confront our own demons and so take delight in finding them mirrored in others – for instance, their thoughtless behaviour of having the music too loud may mirror our own thoughtless behaviour towards our partner.

The word 'quarrel' comes from the Latin *querella*, meaning 'a complaint'. When we quarrel, then, it is an indication that we are finding fault or complaining to another source that the world is not operating according to our perceived needs.

The three build-up phases to quarrelling

Firstly, we start with having a need or desire. **Secondly,** we have the reaction or outcome to this need that we anticipate getting from others. **Thirdly,** there is our own, typical reaction to the outcome.

Let's take the example of your anniversary.

We (1) **start** with wanting our partner to remember our anniversary and make us feel special and loved. That's our **need**.

Then we have the (2) **anticipated outcome** to that need which will depend on our emotional inventory – what we have come to expect from relationships in general. If, for instance, our history has been one of being rejected or of others being insensitive to our needs, this will determine the outcome we expect. In this case, we would expect our partner to be insensitive and to reject us, because that is what happens (we have learnt) in relationships. So, the day arrives and, in contrast to our need, our partner does not seem to have remembered.

We (3) **respond** in a manner that we normally adopt when feeling hurt and rejected – we withdraw into an angry silence and don't speak to our partner or, if we do, what we say carries an odious tone. This inevitably leads to a quarrel and the pattern of fighting that we have become accustomed to is repeated.

On the other hand, perhaps our history was not one of rejection and feeling hurt. If, for instance, we had experienced love and acceptance as children and adults, then our outcome and response would differ greatly. Instead of expecting our needs not to be met, and in so doing creating scenario after scenario of rejection and hurt followed by a quarrel, we would expect love and acceptance. Even if our partner was prone to forget, we would gently remind him/her prior to the event and understand that it was not a lack of love that caused the oversight, but rather a simple slip of the mind, which we all experience from time to time. Alternatively, we might take it upon ourselves to show our love and caring by planning something special ourselves as a surprise for our partner, rather than expect them to do so – we would treat them in a manner in which we would like to be treated.

Therefore, it is our emotional make-up that creates the outcome – we sabotage our need or desire with our past and present expectations. We project what we expect into any number of relationships and in so doing create the disappointing outcome. So, to stop a pattern of quarrelling in relationships, we have to own and identify our emotional inventory. Do you expect to be loved, to be respected, to feel good about who you are, to be understood and listened to? If you do not answer 'yes' to all of these questions, then see that it is your expectation of not receiving this treatment that is the cause of the disappointing outcome. When you encounter the pattern that you have created, it pushes the same buttons that say, 'I am not worthy of being loved, respected, having self-worth, being understood or listened to.' Naturally, when that happens you will feel sad and hurt which causes you to respond in anger.

To change the quarrelsome pattern, then, you have to work with issues of self-worth – respecting yourself, listening to your own inner voice and so on. Yet rather than do this, because it is hard and takes great courage, we lash out at the other person and blame them.

Sulking

Sulking is a form of passive aggressive behaviour. The person who sulks lacks the self-confidence and personal power to confront the person with whom they are angry. Instead, they avoid conflict and withdraw emotionally, yet still harbour the resentment and anger. Typically, any questions from the person they are angry with, as to why they are angry, are met with a denial that they are indeed angry or else a sullen silence.

The word 'sullen' ultimately comes from the Latin *solus*, meaning 'alone'. If we take the root meaning of the word as indicative of its underlying emotional meaning, then when we are sullen, we show that we are not only passively resentful, but are actually feeling very alone. The world is a place where we perceive that no one actually understands us. We all want to be understood and empathized with. When we do not experience this, it creates a feeling of being alone in a place where our pain is not comprehended or even acknowledged. By emotionally withdrawing ourselves and becoming unresponsive, we ensure that others can't relate to us and so we sabotage our own need for intimacy.

We want intimacy and understanding yet, rather than reach out, we withdraw. It is a watery or feminine response, as opposed to a fiery or masculine reaction, where we might lash out in anger. As with quarrelling, we have, through our emotional wounds, envisaged an expected outcome to which, when it transpires, we respond in a way typical of us i.e. passive aggressive withdrawal. For a person who feels less powerful in a relationship, this is a wonderfully manipulative tool to bring the person with more power to their guilty knees.

Take the example of Joan, a dynamic, fiery, sports coach and her husband Ben, a quiet, reserved advertising copywriter. Every time Joan asks him to do something around the house, Ben's response is to say yes, but do nothing, which drives Joan crazy. Aware that she may be nagging him, she tries not to insist that he helps around the house, yet this makes her angry when he contributes very little. Eventually, her anger breaks through her attempts not to nag and she asks him to do a particular chore. He, sensing her anger, and yet feeling resentful about her request, does not do it, which makes her even angrier. The more he continues either not to do the task or to delay it, the angrier she becomes. Unable to confront her anger, he withdraws emotionally and sulks. By withdrawing, he forces her to pander to him, if her need to be intimate is to be met. Yet the more she tries to be 'nice', the more he ignores her attempts. He now has the upper hand, as he is pulling her strings and forcing her to come to him. Although he lacks the ability to tell her what is upsetting him, he has found a way to manipulate her into feeling guilty. So long as he plays this card, he feels in control. If he stops sulking he is back to feeling inadequate and disempowered.

Ben's need is to be appreciated for what he does do, in terms of the home. He feels he works long hours and therefore wants to put his feet up and relax at home. Joan works mornings only and her contribution to the finances of the household is considerably smaller. Ben feels justified, then, in doing less in the home – a pattern he learnt from his parents. His expected outcome on his return from work, however, is to be nagged and made to feel useless. His response is then to withdraw as described. By carrying a history of feeling inadequate, Ben sets himself up for this outcome. When it manifests, it pushes him into anger which, feeling disempowered, he is unable to deal with appropriately – such as discussing how he feels about the situation with Joan. Instead, he seeks for ways to empower himself, which he does by withdrawing so that she is forced to reach out and, by doing so, make herself more vulnerable.

Another example is when we ask someone to help in some way, such as by washing the dishes. This makes them angry, as perhaps they do not feel they need or want to and so they respond by 'accidentally' breaking a precious plate. Instead of simply saying 'No, I washed up at lunch,' they perform the task with masked aggression.

We expect people to know and understand what is going on inside us without our having to convey any message. When they fail to, we get angry. Feeling helpless, abused, ineffectual and misunderstood, their response or lack of it only serves to push old childhood buttons and confirm these feelings of ours. We then focus our anger on to them, and punish them, rather than explore why we feel this way and work at rewriting this learnt program. It is, however, a highly effective response, which is why we use it often to gain control of a situation and get our way.

The trouble is that, even when conversation is resumed, the actual incident that started the war is seldom discussed. Left to fester, it moves our relationship from one of intimacy to one of co-dependency. John Gray, author of *What You Feel You Can Heal*, describes this deterioration in four stages: resisting, resenting, rejection and repression.[3]

When **resisting**, we hold back from communicating openly for fear of being ridiculed or made to feel worthless. This leads to **resentment** in not being able to share ourselves completely. We then **reject** the other person, through sulking and withdrawing. Finally, we appear to get over it and make-up yet, in not expressing the cause of our initial anger, we **repress** our true feelings. In time, the relationship deteriorates to the point that we repress all feelings, positive and negative, and we find ourselves cohabiting with someone we barely seem to know. We have created such barriers that there is no room for intimacy or understanding. It is interesting that the word 'intimacy' sounds like 'into me see.' Where there is no understanding ('into me see') there can be no intimacy.

A friend used to use this approach. When asked if there was a problem, the standard response would be 'No, nothing's the matter.' (**Resisting**). Feeling hugely **resentful** because of what he perceived to be the problem, he would **reject** us by withdrawing and sulking, to the point that the **repressed** anger was tangible in the air. After years of being made to feel guilty, we rebelled against this and stopped feeling any guilt. With this breakthrough came a complete breakdown in any hope of a meaningful relationship, as we all repressed what we felt and consequently there could be no depth or closeness of any kind. All hope of intimacy was smashed and the relationship moved to one of polite indifference.

How to identify it, how to stop it... and why we don't want to

Ask yourself how able you are to truthfully express your feelings, particularly anger, to another person. Can you address them calmly and say, 'What you are doing makes me feel angry, because it feels to me as if you are abusing me'? or, 'by ignoring my needs, you make me feel unloved and worthless'? Do you rather get in a huff and not say anything, yet take your revenge by making them suffer? Why would you not want to stop this and enter into a more honest relationship? The answer is simple: sulking gives you power when you feel disempowered -who would voluntarily want to give that up?

Sulking allows you to control and manipulate situations. Whenever we have little self-worth, we will always try to gain control of situations or people through manipulative means. Stopping sulking, then, involves working with issues of self-worth and building the self so that we have inner or true power. Then we will not have to try to create external power by manipulating others through guilt.

Start working with communicating openly with others, at the first hint of anger. The other person may not particularly enjoy what you have to say but, given the other option of being made to feel guilty for days, speaking about the problem is infinitely preferable.

Endnotes

1 Yoga sutras 11:36

2 Holy Bible. St James Edition. John 1:1

3 Gray, John, *What You Feel You Can Heal,* Harper Audio, San Francisco, 1995.

Chapter Fourteen
Habits that harm

Habits that seriously affect our lives

Every time we light up a cigarette, eat a Buster Burger with extra cheese, have another cup of coffee, eat an entire slab of chocolate or indulge in a wild drinking binge, we are harming ourselves. Yet, for most people, in spite of overwhelming proof that these do cause physical harm, these behaviours are fairly acceptable. In truth, most of us indulge in at least one of these behaviours regularly. Why? Because they make us feel good while we are doing them, even though we know that we'll have a hangover, weight problems, increase the risk of heart disease and so on. Sometimes guilt drives us to perform these habits secretly, such as having a smoke while your wife's out, or hiding all evidence of the chocolate wrapping.

Why, then, do we raise our eyebrows when someone harms themselves through cutting themselves or pulling out their hair? Because it's the obvious desire to hurt ourselves that is hard to deal with. When someone has cuts all the way up their arm, we cannot deny the emotional pain they are in, whereas, when we drink too much, we use denial as a means to avoid facing or admitting that there is a real, underlying emotional issue.

Much of this chapter revolves around women and their lack of a positive self-image. Perhaps it is due to years of bombardment through the media of retouched perfected images of what 'true' women should look like which results in an extremely low self-image, often to the point of self-hatred. Our own perceived, inferior, image seems so far removed from this that we constantly berate ourselves for not being skinny enough, for being blemished, having cellulite, lacking appropriate firmness, having incorrectly-sized boobs … the list is endless. Couple this with instability and often abuse in the home life and the problem is compounded.

From super model to superstar, very few women ever believe that they are perfect, simply as they are. As traditional home life disintegrates, abuse increases and the role of religion diminishes – no wonder the habits mentioned in this chapter are on the increase.

Self-harming

What is self-harming?

> *Self-harming is a way of dealing with emotional pain in a physical way – like screaming without opening your mouth.*[1]

Samaritans' spokesperson

Dear Ms Gadd,

This is the first time I've ever told anybody about what I do. From a very young age I have bitten my nails, my cheeks, pulled my eyelashes and scratched and picked at my skin. Some days, for no reason it seems, I will pull all of my eyelashes out. Another day I'll chew my checks so they bleed and so on. Otherwise I appear quite normal and no one is aware of what I do – not even my husband.

The letter went on to describe how the habit had affected her life and the degree to which it had caused her to have a huge dislike of herself. It was a heart-wrenching appeal for help from someone so far away. To put pen to paper after so many years, to disclose the secret to a complete stranger must have taken enormous amounts of courage.

The letter arrived in response to my previous book, *Healing Habits,* and prompted me to look into the issue in greater depth. Broadly speaking, self-harming is when someone voluntarily inflicts physical pain on themselves – such as through burning, cutting oneself with a razor-blade or pair of scissors etc., pulling one's hair out, picking at the skin, taking small overdoses of pills, or hitting the body with an object or one's own fists. Because it is such a vast topic, I have isolated hair-pulling and skin-picking and handled them separately, although, broadly speaking, they fall under the heading of self-harming and many of the causes and treatments are similar.

Who does it?

More than 24,000 teenagers will be admitted to hospital in the UK each year because they have deliberately harmed themselves. Girls are four times more likely to self-harm than boys.[2] The incidence of self-harming seems to be increasing (according to ChildLine UK, there was an increase of almost 30% during the last year[2]) which could be attributed to an increase in dysfunctional home environments and added pressure leading to greater emotional stress and a lowering of self-esteem. What is disturbing is that the majority of people who self-harm will never receive professional assistance. Some figures quoted by the Samaritans estimate that in the UK as many as one in ten teenagers self-harm, although this figure reduces with the onset of adulthood. The most common method involves cutting, followed by poisoning.[2]

What drives someone to such depths of anguish that they would seek to harm themselves, as a way to alleviate the emotional pain that they are experiencing?

If you are concerned as to whether or not you self-harm, ask yourself:

- Do you deliberately try to cause physical harm to yourself in ways where the damage is visible for some time afterwards?
- When feeling unpleasant or unhappy emotions, do you harm yourself in order to alleviate them?
- Do you often imagine harming yourself even when you are not upset?

If you answered 'yes' to these questions, you will in all likelihood be self-harming and should consider seeking professional help before the problem escalates.

What causes it?

A history of abuse is most often the prime cause, be the abuse emotional, physical or sexual. With the family, religious and society structures crumbling, many teenagers feel very alone when it comes to dealing with emotional problems. Consequently, when faced with incest, rape, school pressures, family conflict, abuse, the death of a loved one, bullying, financial concerns, depression and relationship issues, there is often no one to talk to.

Often dismissed by the ignorant as an attention-seeking ploy, this is rarely the case as the majority of self-harmers are secretive about their habit, with the result that it may go unnoticed by other family members or friends. It is, however, an indication of a serious need for help and understanding.

Self-harmers are often understandably angry at the situation yet feel unable to do anything about it. It may start as a spur of the moment reaction to a build-up of anger and the resulting stress reduction; gradually it becomes **the** way to reduce stress caused by painful emotions and can continue undetected by others for years. Whereas one feels one has little control in the outside world, harming gives one a feeling some degree of control, even it is only to the degree that one wounds oneself. By inflicting pain, self-harmers attempt to regain the power they have lost in their lives. The amount of pain inflicted is not necessarily an indication of how serious the emotional issues are; with time, the person becomes more resilient to pain and so, in order to achieve the same sense of relief, the level of harm needs to increase. Spiralling out of control, then, the problem can result in serious infections and scarring.

The emotional issues

When our emotional pain is so intense that we feel unable to feel or deal with it, harming ourselves physically is a way of coping with it. Actually creating the wound, we feel, is a way of making our unexpressed emotions tangible and real, either as an attempt to confront the issues or to punish ourselves. It is a sign of a deeply distressed person and should never be regarded as simply an attempt to seek attention. The self-harmer's body and inflicted wounds become the mirror for intense emotional pain. In some cases, they may also see it as a way to get their own back on those who have harmed them. Although it is seldom an attempt to commit suicide, people who self-harm are far more likely to commit suicide during their lives.[2] Low self-esteem is always part of the cause and the reason why many self-harmers feel unable to express their feelings to others.

Frequently, self-harmers feel angry and frustrated at not being seen for who they are or truly heard by others. If we don't feel good about who we are, then we are both afraid and feel incapable of having the confidence to share our problems with others. Feeling worthless and disempowered, there appears to be no acceptable way of expressing how we feel to others and we may attempt to negate our feelings. We don't feel worthy of their time or attention, yet are angry at not receiving it.

Girls suffer more sexual abuse than boys, which may also be a contributing factor in the predominance of self-harming in women. Commonly, when we are abused as children, we feel that we are to blame for what has happened and so instead of taking our anger at being violated out on the perpetrator, we turn it inward and harm ourselves. It is an act of extreme self-hatred.

In older women, self-harming can relate to a loss of self; they may have devoted their lives to pleasing others, whilst denying their own needs. This, coupled with an abusive relationship, can lead to intense feelings of worthlessness and consequently a fear of voicing one's feelings. It becomes a way of trying to cope with all the problems in one's life. The distance between pain and pleasure can also become blurred, as in sadomasochism, when what hurts us actually pleases us as well.

Often, in traumatic situations we become numbed emotionally as a means of survival; harming can bring about this same feeling of numbness, making the painful experiences of our lives seem distant, much as we might experience through taking certain drugs.

Guilt and shame are the inevitable companions of self-harming, both in terms of how we are and how we behave. Each fresh cut or burn increases the guilt and shame and so fires our need to self-harm. This is demonstrated in the story of Donald.

Donald was a young man in his early teens who was sent to a new boarding school after his parents' divorce. As with his previous school, he felt estranged from his peers, whom he saw as immature and idiotic. He felt isolated and alone in his love of music and the arts rather than rugby and soccer and was constantly being bullied by other boys who saw his difference as a disability. He started believing that he was indeed odd and so his self-esteem plummeted. At home things weren't much better, as his parents had just come through a messy divorce.

A brief enquiry into the family dynamics showed that his father had constantly criticized Donald, who in his eyes, never matched up to the father's expectations. Sending Donald to boarding school was a way of removing him from being a burden on his mother and ensuring a 'manly' upbringing now that his father was absent.

Unable to talk to anyone about his anguish and anger at being isolated and ridiculed by his classmates, Donald took to long bouts of depressive brooding and all-night reading bouts. He managed to organize a separate room for himself out of the school dormitory and here his self-loathing and emotional pain turned inward, as he began to cut himself with his penknife. The inadequacy and shame he felt at his own weakness for doing so, together with the view he knew his father would take of this behaviour, only increased his need to perform these acts; the situation spiralled out of control until intervention was able to remedy the situation.

Joyce started self-harming later in life. Married at a young age to a man sixteen years her senior, it seemed to Joyce as if she had quickly swapped her school suitcase for a nappy holder, as the first of her four children was born. Ten years later, Joyce had no fond memories of a fun-filled youth; she felt as if she had become an obliging servant to the needs of her demanding family, in particular her husband who, in his controlling rule of her, appeared more as an abusive father figure than a husband. Depression set in together with a complete lack of any sense of self. Behind this there was extreme anger at having lost her youth to a group of people who had little understanding or gratitude for what she had done. The situation at home became intolerable and Joyce began self-harming as a way to express all the pain she felt she could not convey to those whose lives she shared.

Don't we all self-harm?

To some degree, most of us perform certain acts of self-harming: we eat what is unhealthy for us; we drink excessively (although we know it is killing off our brain cells); we allow ourselves to become overworked and stressed; we have relationships which are abusive; we stay in jobs we hate, simply because we feel insecure about the thought of leaving them... the list is endless. Yet all of these acts carry a certain degree of social acceptability and few of us would really regard what we do as harming ourselves intentionally. Yet the truth of the matter is that harming ourselves in the broader context is very common. It is only when it comes to creating actual, visible, physical harm that self-harming seems to have pushed beyond the boundaries of what is acceptable and into what is not.

Dangers

Obviously, harming oneself can result in many negative outcomes, such as infections, permanent scar damage, and the risk that someday, inadvertently, you may go too far and risk killing yourself. Besides the physical harm, the need to lie and cover-up your harming may prove very stressful to maintain.

Tim seemed in every way a normal family man. He had two children, a house and the accompanying mortgage, a good schooling history, a prestigious job as an architect- in fact, nothing to hint at the turmoil that lay beneath his surface.

I had been friends with him and his wife for a number of years. One day I met him and noticed that he had deep, angry, scratches on his face. He told me they were due to his being attacked by robbers, who had held him up and snatched his cellphone. As he sought to fend them off, one of them had gouged his face – a perfectly plausible explanation and one that I believed, until I met his wife, who told quite a different tale.

Tim, it appears, had inflicted the wounds on himself in a fit of rage. Too ashamed to tell the truth, he had invented the story of the thieves. Apparently, Tim had a long history of self-harming. There were stories of his kicking a wall so hard he broke his foot, breaking bones in his hand when hitting a door, as well as taking overdoses of tablets and a history of bad absenteeism from work (always for supposedly legitimate 'accidents' or 'illnesses'). Most people had the impression that he was simply accident-prone and very unlucky.

Prone to bouts of rage, rather than inflict his anger on those close to him, he turned it upon himself. This may sound slightly noble, but for the fact that his children had witnessed his attacks, which had caused them considerable stress and emotional trauma. It was only through being made to realize the effect his actions had on those he loved that Tim made a concerted effort to stop self-harming. In his case, drinking was a key factor. By stopping his drinking, he was able to reduce the intensity of his angry explosions as well as control his reactions.

From hate to love

While counselling and the intervention of a psychologist and/or qualified health professional is recommended, it is possible for a person who self-harms to assume some control over the situation. Like any habit, self-harming has become a learnt way to cope with emotional problems. However, what needs to be understood on the road to recovery is that there are a number of different techniques which can be used to stop harming, all of which may be more or less effective depending on the individual. They include:

- Finding an outlet such as a punch-bag to vent your anger on such as a sport
- Yoga and deep-breathing exercises
- Keeping a journal and recording in it your feelings
- Removing potential self-harming objects from your living area
- Starting to learn to talk to others about how you feel
- Using ice-cubes and holding them – it's painful but not harmful

When dealing with another person who is self-harming, remember not to judge their actions and see them as a negative reflection of yourself. Forcing them to stop because their actions make you feel uncomfortable is obviously not going to achieve a favourable result. What the person needs is support and unconditional acceptance and love, as opposed to recriminations and criticism.

Hair-pulling

What is it?

Is life stressing you to the point that you are literally *pulling your hair out?* Trichotillomania (TTM) or hair-pulling is behaviour that causes people to pull out their hair from the head, eyebrows, eyelashes, underarms or pubic region. It has been classified as a habit, an addiction, a tic, obsessive compulsive disorder and, most commonly, impulse control disorder (similar to kleptomania or stealing compulsively).

Normally, there is an increase in emotional tension just before the urge to pull arises or when the person attempts to resist doing so. Obviously, the results are unsightly, yet the urge to pull is stronger than the fear of the resulting unsightly baldness. This causes significant distress in all areas of one's life.

The amount people pull varies considerably from person to person, as does the compulsion to pull. Most often, they will go to great lengths to cover their bald spots, with scarves, wigs, hats or make-up. At times, they may be reticent to interact with others for fear that their problem will be exposed. Teenagers who are particularly concerned with their appearance may suffer particularly.

Hair-pulling was not really known in the media until the early 1990s and, even today, there are many people who have little knowledge about the problem from which they suffer – nor about any treatment.

Some hair-pullers pull out their hair one strand at a time, examining it before pulling another. They may also chew the hair and, in some cases, actually eat it. Other harming habits, such as self-harming, skin-picking or scratching and nail-biting (see Chapter Six) can also become part of the habitual practice. Some may have symptoms of Obsessive Compulsive Disorder (see Chapter Three) such as compulsive washing, checking, counting etc. Depression is also an issue, though it is not known if this is a cause or result of the problem.

Who does it?

Most commonly, hair-pulling starts in children around the age of twelve[3] and, consequently, is thought to be associated with pubertal hormonal changes. Hair-pulling can also start much earlier or later in life. Like all habits that harm, a stressful event can be linked to its onset, such as a death in the family, change of schools, conflict or abuse. It affects between one to two percent of the population, with the majority of hair-pullers being girls (roughly 90%, although this may not be accurate as it is suspected that men seldom seek treatment and therefore the statistics are not gender accurate).[3] It is also more common in teenagers than in other age groups.

Hair and its relevance

In the Bible, Samson's hair was symbolic of his strength and holiness: *If my hair were cut, I should lose my strength and be as weak as anyone else.*[4] Now, obviously it was not his hair, as such, that gave him strength, but rather what it symbolized – namely, his connection to God. This connection gave him his charismatic power.

The Native American Indians also regarded their hair as their link to spirit, hence their feathered headdresses which were a way to enhance this connection. In scalping a defeated enemy, the warrior removed his victim's hair and consequently his ability to reconnect with the Great Spirit after death. As hair grows from the seventh energetic body, in the Eastern tradition, it is also seen as a sort of antenna into the astral and mental planes. For instance, Hasidic Jews do not cut their hair – seeing it as lines of force connecting them to the universe and God.

When taking their vows, nuns have their hair cut or shaved off, as symbolic of a new way of life and submission to God. Many other monks in various religions, such as the Chinese Manchus, do the same. In India, as part of a particular cult's annual ceremony, disciples are required to crawl many kilometres on their knees to a temple, where their hair is roughly (and painfully) pulled out by priests, as a means of purification.

The first thing that happens when a new recruit enters the military is that his hair gets shorn. By doing this, he is stripped of his personal power and strength as an individual. Likewise, the Neo-Nazi movement has shaven heads as an identifying symbol. Here, the relationship to the gang and its strength and doctrine become more important than the individual's needs and personal power.

Shining hair is indicative of a healthy body, while loss of hair results from tension and lack of enjoyment i.e. feeling unconnected to the Divine in our lives. Often, when we cut or change the colour of our hair or its style, we demonstrate visibly the change that has (or we hope will) occurred in our lives.

Calling a difficult, scary situation a *hairy* or *hair-raising* experience indicates that the event required us to draw in strength from the Divine. As our *hair stood on end,* we sought to summon extra power to get us through the situation. In contrast, *letting one's hair down* meant forsaking one's spiritual connection in order to seek earthly pleasures for which the remedy the following morning would be the *hair of the dog that bit you!* There is also a sexual aspect to this phrase, coming from ancient times when a woman's loose hair signified virginity or being single/available. *Letting your hair down,* then, is also connected to letting go of your sexual inhibitions.

Emotional causes

While shame and guilt must be the overriding result of hair-pulling, tension and frustration are its cause. The link with the onset of puberty may relate to the frustration one feels at this age, of not being able to express one's thoughts and feelings fully for fear of being ridiculed. You may have an opinion, but be afraid to express it for fear that it may cause confrontation, so you negate your own desires in order to avoid conflict. Having a low-self esteem, you may also feel that your opinions and feelings are of little worth anyway. However, when we can't express who we are, it creates a backlog of frustration. Girls, being typically less fiery than their male counterparts, may battle with this problem more, as boys may have more physical/sporting outlets for their frustration.

These two aspects – guilt and shame – confirm our own inadequacies. We feel flawed and therefore afraid to voice who we really are, for fear that those shortcomings will be revealed. Our shame then acts as an inner critic, telling us that we aren't worthy of being heeded or listened to, that we aren't bright enough, pretty enough or knowledgeable enough for our needs to be expressed or met. Our guilt and shame about our hair-pulling, then, confirms this assumption.

This original feeling of being flawed may have resulted from almost any kind of abuse as a child – be it neglect, abandonment, excessive criticism, inappropriate boundaries, emotional or sexual abuse, or an extremely authoritarian upbringing. Often, a parent's shame may be transferred to a child when he or she fails to live up to his or her need for approval and the child is then shamed for this. We then see *ourselves*, as opposed to what we do, as flawed and, afraid of further humiliation, give in to others in order to maintain peace. Our lives are then an attempt to please others, which means repressing our own needs.

Feeling inadequate, everything we do in life simply reaffirms and creates this belief system. However, constantly giving in to the will of others at the expense of our own creates huge tension which we relieve through hair-pulling. Where we choose to pull indicates where we are feeling repressed and frustrated. Hair on the head relates to one's ideas and thoughts, hair in the pubic region to one's sexual feelings, hair on the eyebrows to control and expressive issues, while eye-lashes relate to frustration at others' not seeing who we really are.

From bald to beautiful – healing strategies

Conventional treatment involves Cognitive-Behavioural Therapy[5] taught by a specially-trained psychologist; people are taught to identify the triggers that result in hair-pulling and then to substitute or re-direct the impulse with other, less harmful habits. Some people have had success by simply interrupting their hair-pulling – such as by putting bandages on their fingers or keeping records or journals of their need to pull and when and how it is triggered. Medically, some individuals have found that selective serotonin re-uptake inhibitors (such as Prozac) have eliminated the desire to pull (for some hair-pullers, this method reduced the urge, while for others there was no effect at all). Support groups have helped others, simply by knowing that they were not alone.

Alternative therapies include hypnotherapy, the martial arts, exercise, dietary changes, assertiveness programs, yoga, meditation for stress release, and psychotherapy to release frustration and shame, as well as strengthening the self-esteem and will.

The encouraging news is that, with proper intervention, most people are eventually able to stop the impulse that results in hair-pulling.

Skin picking

What is it?

Self-injurious skin-picking, or SISP, is the habit of repeatedly scratching, picking or digging into the skin, often to remove small irregularities, and is closely linked with self-harming. Most people use their fingers or nails, while some may use pins, tweezers etc.[5] In severe cases it can result in bad scarring and infection. As with hair-pulling, skin-picking seems to result from a build-up of emotional stress and anxiety, which is relieved through picking. It is also a habit that involves much shame and guilt, which is why people seldom admit that they do it and seek help.

Who does it?

Studies reveal that up to 4% of college students and 2% of dermatology patients pick their skin to the degree where they cause significant scarring and, like hair-pulling, it seems to be on the increase. As with all the harmful behaviours in this chapter, women predominate. A 1998 study by Sabine Wilhelm and her colleagues found that 87% of skin-pickers were women, with nearly half of those being married, and with 74% of them having either finished college or a degree. The average age at which the picking started was 15 although, like other self-harming behaviours, it tended to increase and decrease depending on circumstances. 39% of the people in this study had suffered from acne or a related skin problem when the behaviour began and as many as half had other family members who also skin picked.[5]

The skin and its emotional relevance

The skin is the biggest organ in the body and as such it covers a variety of functions, such as defending us against infection, excreting toxins and controlling our body temperature through perspiring. However, its overriding theme is that of boundaries and how we interact with the outside world. Through it, we express much of our innermost being – through blushing with shame, going red with anger, white and sweating with fear, getting gooseflesh when we are afraid and looking rosy and glowing when we are healthy. Through touch of skin, we relate to others, either being repelled or aroused by them. We also experience intimacy on a deeper level than verbally, and yet this touch can also make us feel vulnerable.

Whatever we see on the skin is a mirror of an inner process, which is why the more skin we reveal the more vulnerable and exposed our inner feelings become. One is far more vulnerable standing naked in front of a stranger than clothed.

In lie-detector tests, every nuance of the skin is electronically monitored to determine the truth of a person's statements. It's rather like carrying a large screen around with you on which, for those perceptive enough to watch, your emotions and thoughts are displayed. Naturally, when it comes to our face, which is the most visible aspect of our skin, we often spend huge amounts of money enhancing its features, through surgery and make-up, to project an image of what we would like to be inside us so that we don't *lose face!*

If we do not like who we are internally, we will constantly try to enhance what we look like externally. Through picking our skin, we want to remove every blemish we find, both internally and externally. Yet doing so causes further blemishing and so the process must continue (in our minds) if we are ever to reach perfection.

Emotional causes

The skin, as mentioned, consists primarily of boundary and communication-related aspects. Digging or picking into it is a way of getting to what's *under our skin* i.e. what's bugging us. Doing it provides immense gratification and pleasure as we expose what was hidden, such as a substance from a pore or lump. This picking relieves boredom, anxiety, sadness and emotional stress.

Issues with the skin are an indication that we do like what we are showing to the world about ourselves. We somehow want or feel that we should be less flawed and so we seek to rectify the problem by picking at our faults, which makes us feel better while we are doing it, but guilty and shameful afterwards.

It is an indication of how much we dislike ourselves and how remote and removed we feel from those around us, who we fear showing the real us, in case they too share our sentiments that we are worthless.

Growing skin – healing processes

The treatments are similar to those for other self-harmful habits. Cognitive-Behavioural Therapy[5] is commonly used as a means to understand the emotional triggers to this problem. Once these are understood, alternative coping strategies are taught. Using gloves, bandages etc. is a way to reduce the sensory input that is part of picking. Stoppicking.com is a web-based program which involves a daily commitment that aims to help you to reach a greater understanding of the problem and to work to heal it.

Any programs which involve working to improve self-image and esteem will benefit, as will therapy to work with self-acceptance, releasing shame and guilt, and developing one's will. Healing is possible and, although there may be the occasional regression, in view of the physical and emotional detrimental effects, it should be encouraged. Working with an organization or professional individual is much easier in most cases than trying to solve the problem on your own, which is why it's advisable to get help.

Shop-lifting

Millions of pounds are spent each year in an attempt to stop people from shop-lifting; in the USA, shop-lifting costs the public over $33 billion per year.[6] Yet, in spite of hi-tech equipment, the problem persists. Shop-lifting has been cited as a major cause of the failure of smaller retail stores and the incidence seems to be increasing.

I once worked for a company which sold sporting goods. One day, shop-lifters managed to walk out of the shop undetected with an entire four foot metal clothes rack on which was hanging an assortment of expensive, sporting fashion items.

The profile of a shop-lifter is varied; there is no set profile in terms of age, race, sex or economic background, although a higher percentage (25%) of shop-lifters are teenagers.[7]

It occurs as a result of:

- Professional activity – shop-lifting as a means of earning a living
- Thrill-seeking
- Feeling entitled – the government/world/company owes me a living
- Social/economic responses – when people can't afford certain items
- Habitual shop-lifting
- A reaction to certain psychological problems, as in kleptomania

For each type of shop-lifter, then, there is a different underlying cause. However, the resulting repercussions in terms of jail sentencing make little differentiation between the various types.

The professionals

Professional shop-lifters understandably aim for high-priced items and frequently know exactly what they want to steal on walking into a store. They may shop-lift as an alternative to working, or perhaps to support an addiction e.g. to drugs. They will normally have a number of networks through which they can sell what they have stolen. They may well resist arrest and show little remorse for their actions. Interestingly, there are a number of websites written by professional shop-lifters who, as their writing demonstrates, clearly see their chosen profession as carrying a high degree of status.

The thrill seekers

Teenagers mostly fall into this group, where what you steal is not as important as the act of stealing itself. Getting away with stealing brings not only status within one's peer group, but also a type of giddy thrill. They may not necessarily go into a store with the intention to shop-lift, but may do so if the opportunity arises, as a way to obtain items that they can't afford or to improve their status amongst their peers.

The 'entitlement shoppers'

Entitlement shoppers feel special – as if society's rules don't apply to them. They believe themselves to be above other people. Laws, rules and accepted norms are the yoke which others must bear, not them. They live in a world oblivious to the burden which they create for others – in this case, increased prices due to the huge amounts stolen. They are often people who have come from backgrounds of wealth and indulgence, where boundaries never existed. Whatever they wanted, they received. They were seldom required to take responsibility for their actions and so developed into selfish, impulsive and immature adults.

Into this category also fall the people who feel that, because they have paid for a hotel room, it is their right to walk off with a proportion of its contents. They may be horrified to be arrested and may try to justify their actions.

Socio-economic issues

In contrast to the typical 'entitlement shopper', some people may have been deprived of attention, material requirements and love as children. As adults, then, they feel entitled to take whatever they require in compensation for what they did not receive as children.

In poorer, disenfranchised communities, where there is a big difference between the haves and the have-nots, people who have not had equal access to education and job opportunities may believe that they are entitled to take that which they cannot afford. It is simply a means of survival.

The habitual shop-lifter

Just as a smoker wants to smoke, or a gambler needs to gamble, a habitual shop-lifter needs to steal to the point that not stealing is equivalent to telling an alcoholic not to drink. For them, stealing is both a thrill and an opportunity to take revenge on a society which they perceive has failed or wronged them. What they steal is often irrelevant; the thrill comes from getting their own back. Unfortunately, this thrill can become addictive and what started out as a bit of a lark can become more permanent, as they seek to recreate the initial high.

Huge amounts of repressed anger and frustration, as well as other stresses and emotional pressures, are found to be relieved by stealing. The stress then builds again until the next item is stolen. In this way, stealing becomes a habitual means of reducing negative, unexpressed emotions.

Kleptomania

Kleptomaniacs act on impulse, i.e. they do not plan to steal and commonly take items for which they have little use. Only 5% of people who shop-lift fall into this category, with women of around 35 years of age being the greatest perpetrators. This behaviour is more a response to emotional turmoil and is not motivated by revenge or need. Frequently, kleptomaniacs suffer from other psychiatric disorders, such as major depression and anxiety. There is some evidence to suggest that abnormalities in serotonin, a chemical found in the brain, may be a cause.[8] They may experience little or no guilt for their actions and surprise at all the fuss if they are caught. They may also experience tension which is relieved by stealing.

Favourite ways of stealing

The open bag is about the most common method used for stealing; other shop-lifters are more inventive, using prams and umbrellas into which to slip items. Newspapers are also handy for smaller items, as is 'crotch-walking' whereby the item is slipped between the thighs and the perpetrator walks out of the shop undetected. Everything from typewriters to hams have been stolen with this technique! Another method is to emerge from the changing booths wearing several more layers of clothing than when you entered.

More brazen thieves simply take what they want, relying on the fear and slow response of shop staff in order to get away with their contraband. On a stand at an expo, several computers were stolen, only a few feet from the owners. In another instance, under the watchful glare of spotlights at the launch of a top-brand luxury car, shop-lifters were able to remove various parts of the car and walk away undetected.

How to stop

Realize that what you are doing is very harmful. Should you be caught, you may face a prison sentence or community service. Then, if it is revenge that you are seeking, society will have the last say. Stealing is no way to retaliate against a society where the law is upheld. If you are tempted, visualize yourself being apprehended and the effect that this would have on yourself and on those you love. There may be underlying problems, such as depression, that are provoking your stealing response. Get help before you are caught. Another suggestion is to find another positive activity to replace stealing.

Endnotes

1 From a summary of research commissioned by Samaritans and carried out by the Centre for Suicide Research, University of Oxford.

2 National Enquiry into self-harm told of worrying upsurge of ChildLine calls on eve of first report. News release 6 Sept.2004 from www.mentalhealth.org.uk Resources: www.nhsdirect.nhs.uk www.selfharm.UK.org, The National Children's Bureau: www.ncb.org.uk, www.mind.org.uk, ChildLine UK 08001111 or www.childline.org.uk, Samaritans: 08457 909090, ParentLine Plus: 0808800 2222

3 Trichotillomania Learning Centre, Inc. www.trich.org

4 Holy Bible: St James version Judges 15 ch.16:15

5 Research by Sabine Wilhelm and colleagues Massachusetts General Hospital and Harvard Medical School in 1998 from www.stoppicking.com

6 2002 National Retail Security Survey from www.crimedoctor.com/shoplifting.htm

7 kidshealth.org/teen/school_jobs/ good_friends/shoplifting.html

8 www.psychnet-uk.com/dsm_iv/kleptomania.htm

Bibliography

Bennett-Goteman, Tara, *Emotional Alchemy,* Rider, London, 2003

Campbell, Don, *The Mozart Effect,* Hodder Mobius, London, 1997

Chopra, Deepak, M.D. *Overcoming Addictions,* Rider, New York, 1997

Chopra, Deepak M.D. *Perfect Health – The complete mind/body guide.* Bantam, London, 1990

Covey, Steven R. *The Seven Habits of Highly Effective People,* Simon and Schuster, New York, 1989

Dethlefsen, Thorwald & Rudiger Dahlke MD, *The Healing Power of Illness,* Element, Shaftesbury, 1992

Evans, Philip, *The Family Medical Reference Book,* Time Warner Books, London, 2003

Gray, John, PhD, *What You Feel You Can Heal,* Harper Audio, New York, 1995

Johnson, Robert A., *Owning Your Own Shadow,* Harper Collins, New York, 1993

Linn, Denise, *Pocketful of Dreams,* Triple Five Publishing, Brighton-le-sands, Australia, 1998

Hay, Louise, *Heal Your Body,* Hay House, Inc., Carlsbad, CA, 2001

Hay, Louise, *You can Heal your Life,* Hay House, Inc., Carlsbad, CA, 2001

Holbeche, Soozi, *The Power of your Dreams,* Piatkus, London, 1991

Judith, Anodea, *Eastern Body Western Mind,* Celestial Arts, Berkeley, California 1996

Jung, Carl, *Man and his Symbols,* Picador, London, 1978

Kornfield, Jack, *After the Ecstasy the Laundry,* Rider, London, 2000

Kübler-Ross, Elisabeth, *On Death and Dying,* Scribner, London, 1997

Myss, Caroline, PhD, *Anatomy of the Human Spirit,* Bantam, London, 1997

Myss, Caroline, PhD, *Sacred Contracts,* Harmony Books, New York, 2001

Ponce, Charles, *Working the Soul,* North Atlanta Books, Berkeley, California, 1988

Rechtschaffen, Stephan, *Time Shifting,* Rider, London, 1996

Roberts, Ron & Sammut, Judy, *Asthma, an Alternative Approach,* Souvenir Press (E&A) Ltd London, 1996

Sharma, Dr R, (Editor) *The* Element *Family Encyclopedia of Health*, Element Books, Shaftsbury, 1998

Sacks, Oliver, *An Anthropologist on Mars* Random House Audio, Unabridged edition 1995

Sabatini, Sandra, *Breath, the Essence of Yoga,* Thorsons, London, 2000

Sagan, Carl, *Broca's Brain,* Hodder & Stoughton, London,1980

Stone, Joshua David, PhD. *Soul Psychology*, Ballantine Wellspring, New York, 1999

Tannahill, Reay, *Sex in History,* Abacus, London, 1981

Thondup, Tulku, *The Healing Power of the Mind*, Shambhala, Boston, 1996

Wauters, Ambika, *Chakras and their Archetypes*, Piatkus, London, 1998

Index

FINDHORN
Press

For a complete Findhorn Press catalogue, please contactct

Findhorn Press
305a The Park
Findhorn, Forres IV36 3TE
Scotland, Great Britain
tel +44 (0)1309-690582
fax + 44 (0)1309-690036
email info@findhornpress.com

or consult our website **www.findhornpress.com**